West to the Pacific

The Story of the Lewis and Clark Expedition

Written and Illustrated
by
Ronald K. Fisher

Edited by
Dr. Merle Wells, Idaho Historical Society

Alpha Omega, Coeur d'Alene, Idaho

Copyright ©1989 by Ronald K. Fisher

All rights reserved. Reproduction of this book, in whole or in part, is prohibited.

Library of Congress Catalog Card Number: 88-72198

ISBN: 0-941734-01-3

Cover: Detail from
"Lewis and Clark at Three Forks"
by E.S. Paxson.
Courtesy of the Montana Historical Society.
Cover design by Linda Roark.

First Paperback Printing 1989
Second Printing 1992

Published by Alpha Omega, Coeur d'Alene, Idaho

Printed and bound in the United States of America
by BookCrafters, Chelsea, Michigan,
and Action Printers, Coeur d'Alene, Idaho.

West to the Pacific
The Story of the Lewis and Clark Expedition

Ronald K. Fisher

For my mom, Myrtle A. Fisher, without whose love, support, and encouragement this book would never have been written. And in memory of my dad, Kenneth L. Fisher.

Table of Contents

1. The Adventure Begins 1
2. A Narrow Escape 9
3. Winter at Fort Mandan 17
4. Challenging the Missouri 27
5. The Great Falls 37
6. Return to the Land of the People 43
7. Cameahwait 53
8. Lolo Pass and Beyond 59
9. On to the Pacific 65
10. Fort Clatsop 73
11. A Matter of Honesty 83
12. Back to the Bitterroots 89
13. Danger Along Marias River 99
14. A Near-Fatal Mistake 109
15. Smoke Signals Near the Yellowstone 113
16. Home Again 121
    Epilogue 129
    Index 139

Chapter 1

The Adventure Begins

Thomas Jefferson, the third President of the United States, was a remarkable man with many interests and abilities. In addition to being a skillful politician and diplomat, he was an agriculturalist, archaeologist, inventor, and author. He possessed an endless fascination with nature. He was eager to know how different types of plants and animals lived, how natural resources could best be preserved and utilized, and how fossils revealed secrets of past life on earth.

When Jefferson became President in 1801, the United States included the land from the Atlantic Ocean in the east to the Mississippi River in the west. Jefferson dreamed that one day his country would become one of the largest, most powerful nations of the world. He wanted America to expand westward to the Pacific Ocean. He hoped that in addition to the obvious increase in size, western expansion and exploration might also yield a new water route across North America. This would allow the United States to become wealthy by facilitating trade in the rich, Oriental market.

Jefferson already knew that a major river known as the Missouri joined the Mississippi from the west. He had also learned that Captain Robert Gray had explored part of another large river that emptied directly into the Pacific Ocean. Gray had named this river the Columbia after his ship and had claimed the land bordering it for the United States. Jefferson thought that perhaps these three great waterways, the Missouri, the Mississippi, and the Columbia, might be used to form a northwest passage across North America. If this proved true, American crews could load their ships in St. Louis and travel almost nonstop all the way to the Pacific and beyond.

Other countries also had plans for the unclaimed parts of North America. Spain had taken possession of the large section of land between the Mississippi River and the Rocky Mountains. This area was known as the Louisiana Territory. However, the Spanish king had difficulty holding onto this enormous area which was located so far from his own country.

In 1800, the King of Spain gave up ownership of Louisiana to the ambitious French leader, Napoleon. This alarmed Jefferson and the American people. The United States had fought the Revolutionary War in 1775 to escape the rule of kings. Now, the Americans' closest neighbor was France, under the imperial command of Napoleon. Who could tell what lay ahead once the French were firmly established on their new land. Jefferson worried about losing access to the area between the Appalacian Mountains and the Mississippi River. This was America's only outlet to world markets via the Mississippi and the port of New Orleans. Matters became even more intense when Jefferson learned that Napoleon was preparing to send an army to secure his hold on Louisiana.

Jefferson decided to take action. He let it be known that the United States would ally itself with England and fight the French if it became necessary. He also sent representatives to France to negotiate the purchase of New Orleans.

The President's representatives were able to purchase far more than the port of New Orleans. Napoleon realized he could not hold the area against England's sea power. He also could not stop Americans from traveling west since they greatly outnumbered the French in the New World. After he lost most of his Caribbean army due to battle and yellow fever, he needed money badly. Napoleon decided to sell all of Louisiana to the United States. Jefferson was able to buy the entire area for 15 million dollars. This was an incredible bargain at only about three cents an acre. The Louisiana Purchase doubled the size of America and provided a major step toward the realization of the President's goal for his country.

Thomas Jefferson   **Napoleon**

America now extended from the Atlantic Ocean to the Rocky Mountains. Between the Rockies and the Pacific Ocean lay the Oregon Country. The United States would have to claim this land also before Jefferson's dream could become reality.

The Oregon Country included the present states of Washington, Oregon, Idaho, and parts of Montana and Wyoming. It also included a part of Canada. The area is called the Pacific Northwest today. Before 1700, only Indians lived there. After 1700, Spanish sea captains arrived to trade and claim some of the land for Spain. Soon Russia and Great Britain also sent traders and made claims in the area.

The Russians began trapping along the Alaskan coast in 1750. They soon extended their work as far south as the Columbia River.

In 1792, an English captain, George Vancouver, anchored his ship in Puget Sound. He claimed the land for Great Britain.

Also in 1792, Robert Gray made his exploration of the lower Columbia River. He developed an American fur trading business called the Yankee Triangle Trade. Gray bought sea otter pelts from Indians along the coast of the Oregon Country and transported them for sale to China. While in the Orient, he bought tea and other valuable goods which he later sold for increased profits to the Americans.

The wealth to be gained in this trading and exploration encouraged four powerful nations—Spain, Russia, Great Britain, and the United States—in their quest to control and eventually gain possession of the Oregon Country.

President Jefferson began to organize an expedition to explore the Louisiana Territory and the Oregon Country. He hoped that it would provide information to promote American settlement of the far west and enable the United States to take possession of the remaining unclaimed land. Officially he said the purpose of the mission was to do scientific and geographic research. He said nothing about America's interest in claiming the Oregon Country. He did not want other nations to recognize his intentions and step up their own efforts to sieze the land. In February, 1803, Congress approved Jefferson's $2,500 budget for the expedition. However, the total cost would eventually amount to $38,722.

Jefferson needed a great deal of information to persuade Americans to travel west. Settlers wanted descriptions of the land, maps of the best travel routes, and facts about wildlife and Indians they would encounter. Experienced, informed guides were needed to lead families through the wilderness to good locations for settlements.

Jefferson chose his personal secretary, Meriwether Lewis, to lead the expedition. Lewis was an expert woodsman who already knew a great deal about survival in the wilderness. He had also been a successful officer under the command of George Washington. The President sent Lewis to Philadelphia to prepare for his work. He took classes in mathematics, astronomy, botany, and zoology. He learned to care for the health of the men who would follow him. Lewis also learned methods for dealing successfully with the Indians he would encounter in his travels.

Lewis needed help in leading an expedition of this size and importance. In July, 1803, he asked his friend, William Clark, to share his responsibilities. The two men had met in the 1790's while they were in the army. Clark had been Lewis' commanding officer. The personalities of the two men complemented each other well. Lewis was intellectual, introspective, and sometimes even withdrawn. Clark, by contrast, was plain, hearty, cheerful, and outgoing. He knew a great deal about the Indians and enjoyed working with them. Clark's ability to sketch enabled him to produce maps and illustrations for the journals the leaders were asked to keep. Both men had wilderness experience and had proven themselves to be gifted leaders.

Clark discussed Lewis' offer with his brother, General George Rogers Clark. He respected the opinion of this Revolutionary War hero who was 18 years older than himself.

George thought this was an excellent opportunity and encouraged William to accept.

William Clark **Meriwether Lewis**

Lewis was delighted when Clark notified him of his intention to join the expedition. Clark agreed to travel to St. Louis to make final preparations for the journey.

The men made a good team. During the entire expedition they rarely disagreed. There are only two known differences of opinion. First, they failed to agree on the taste of dog meat which Lewis liked and Clark detested. Then, they held separate ideas about the need for salt in the diet. Lewis craved it while Clark remained indifferent.

Lewis had the responsiblity of purchasing the supplies. He selected medicines, scientific instruments, tools, $2,000 worth of gifts for the Indians, 20 barrels of flour, and 7 barrels of salt. He managed to acquire some of the first matches ever made. Lewis also supervised the manufacture of firearms for his men.

The gifts which the captains took for the Indians were very important to the expedition. Lewis and Clark knew that

Indians expected gifts as a sign of friendship. Trade goods were also used as money among Native Americans. The captains took beads, flags, soap, cloth, knives, clothing, and tools. They also took special silver medals to present to important leaders. These medals, known as Jefferson Peace Medals, had a picture of the President on one side and two hands clasped in friendship on the other. They became prized reminders of the white men's visit.

Both Lewis and Clark worked to select and train the men for their expedition. They needed strong, healthy woodsmen who would be able to face many dangers and hardships. Unmarried men were preferred because they had no dependents to worry about if they failed to return.

Over 100 young men volunteered. Some of them were rejected immediately and others were found unsuitable during their training in the winter of 1803-04. The training camp was located across the river from St. Louis. By the spring of 1804, forty- five men had qualified for the expedition.

George Drewyer was chosen to be second in command after Lewis and Clark. In addition to his job as chief scout and interpreter, he was placed in charge of the hunters who provided food for the explorers. Drewyer's skill in using sign language also made him extremely helpful in communicating with the various Indian tribes.

Clark decided to include Ben York, his servant of many years. York was given the responsibility of caring for the camp and his master's personal possessions. His friendly, outgoing personality made him very popular with the Indians most of whom had never seen a black man before.

Lewis took his dog, Scannon, along with him. Scannon was a 160 pound, black Newfoundland. Lewis thought the animal's great size would impress the Indians. Also, Scannon's bark would help keep grizzly bears and other wild animals away from the camp.

Lewis and Clark left St. Louis aboard a keelboat named the Discovery.

The Lewis and Clark Expedition, officially called the Corps of Discovery, left St. Louis on May 14, 1804. They traveled up the river in a 55–foot long keelboat named the Discovery and two smaller pirogues (French-style canoes). They began their journey of nearly 4,000 miles to the Pacific Ocean with this order from President Jefferson:

> The object of your mission is to explore the Missouri River, and such principal stream [sic] of it, as, by its course and communication with the water of the Pacific Ocean may offer the most direct and practicable water communication across the continent for the purpose of commerce.

Chapter 2

A Narrow Escape

The first two months of the expedition provided many valuable learning experiences for the men. They learned to work together as a team and expect rigorous military discipline when they disobeyed their leaders. Together they fought the treacherous Missouri River with its shifting sandbars, crumbling banks, hidden snags, swift currents, and whirling eddies. They faced sudden, fierce storms followed by days of muggy heat without even the hint of a breeze. Some of them suffered from sunstroke and all of them suffered from mosquitoes whose fierce attacks prevented them from sleeping or even standing still at times. The men smeared themselves with bear grease to discourage the bites of these bothersome insects.

Some of the men learned to follow orders the hard way. One received 50 lashes for drinking on duty and another received 100 lashes for falling asleep on watch. The punishments may seem severe but mistakes could prove costly and too many lives were at stake to take careless chances.

Undoubtedly the men had some fun also during this time. They probably laughed, joked, wrestled, and played tricks on one another. One such incident ended with sand being thrown into York's eyes and another ended in a fight. Hunting was good and the men ate well after an exhausting day on the river.

On August 20, the only death on the entire expedition occurred. Sergeant Charles Floyd had become ill two weeks earlier but had seemed to recover. Then, on August 19, the illness returned and became serious. Sergeant Floyd was in great pain and could not keep food or medicine down. It is thought he suffered from an acute attack of appendicitis. Clark stayed up with him most of the night but no improvement was seen. On the morning of the 20th, the captains made Floyd as comfortable as possible aboard their boat and set sail on the river. By late morning, his pulse was so weak it could hardly be felt. As he died, he whispered to Clark, "I'm going away." The men of the expedition sadly buried their friend on the top of a nearby hill. After the service, the captains named a river Floyd's River in his honor.

The men buried the body of their friend, Sergeant Charles Floyd, on a hill beside the river.

The incident served to remind everyone of the seriousness and danger of their mission. They were alone in the wilderness and had only each other to depend upon for their safety. This tragedy bound the members of the expedition more closely together.

As they traveled, Clark recorded each bend in the river, as well as the kinds of plant and animal life they discovered. Jefferson was especially eager to hear about any new animals found on the journey. He had discovered the fossil of a giant ground-sloth (named Megalonyx jeffersoni) which he proudly displayed in the East Room of the White House. The President wondered if this animal might still exist in the unexplored west. Though the captains failed to locate the giant sloth, they did record information about the prairie dog, coyote, white-tailed jackrabbit, western grey wolf, and a new kind of deer which they called a "mule deer" because of its large ears. Journals were filled with information and boxes were loaded with specimens and study skins.

As they traveled on the river, the men looked forward to meeting the various Indian tribes. However, they saw only a few on the first 600 miles of their journey. Most of the Omaha, Pawnee, and Sioux remained hidden. They watched the white travelers and tried to determine whether they were peaceful or warlike.

The few meetings with Indians that did occur during this time were peaceful. Then, in September, the expedition encountered the hostile Teton Sioux.

Lewis and Clark had been warned about these Indians before they left St. Louis. Travelers had told them how Teton warriors blocked passage on the river and demanded huge payments before allowing traders to pass. The captains had also been informed that the Tetons were currently raiding the villages of other Indian tribes.

On September 23, as Lewis and Clark were camped beside

The explorers looked forward to meeting the various Indian tribes as they traveled on the river.

the river, three young Teton boys swam across to them from the opposite bank. The captains wanted a peaceful council with the Sioux and decided to use the boys as messengers to arrange one. Meanwhile, the boats were anchored midstream for protection and a heavy guard posted on shore.

The council was held on a sandbar. The captains began with the presentation of gifts. Clark handed out blankets, coats, and tobacco. The Indians said the gifts were not enough for them to allow passage on the river. They wanted much more. One chief was insulting and Clark became so angry he drew his sword.

Everyone sensed the danger of this situation. The Indians drew their bows and Lewis ordered his men on the boats to prepare to fire. Twelve more men from the expedition quickly joined their leaders on the sandbar for protection. Fearing the white men's more powerful weapons, the Indians withdrew and said they would return the next day to continue the meeting.

That night the captains got little rest as they worried about the safety of their men and the future of their expedition.

In the morning, the Sioux tried a different approach to dealing with the white men. They provided a magnificent feast and entertained the expedition with full honors. They served 400 pounds of excellent buffalo meat, pemmican, and the best parts of roast dog. The captains were carried to the banquet on beautifully painted buffalo robes.

During the entertainment, an Omaha captive of the Sioux managed to deliver a warning. The Tetons were planning to attack the expedition the next day and take all the supplies by force. The feast was only a trick to get the white men off their guard.

The second night was even more restless for the captains than the first had been. Lewis and Clark were determined to continue on their expedition. However, they wanted to prevent the loss of life that could result if the Indians attacked. Since the Tetons wanted all the supplies and trade goods, giving in to their demands was impossible. Without supplies, the expedition could not continue. It seemed there was little choice. They must fight or return to St. Louis. Then Clark got an idea. Perhaps he could plan his own surprise for the Sioux warriors.

In the morning, as the expedition was preparing to leave, the Tetons returned to demand the cargo for right of passage. Clark, who had stationed himself next to the ship's large swivel gun, aimed the weapon into the crowd of warriors and prepared to fire. The Indians were afraid of the gun and backed away from the boat. Clark threw a pouch of tobacco to the chief and ordered his men to sail away.

The Teton Sioux blocked the river and demanded huge payments for right of passage.

Clark aimed the ship's swivel gun at the Teton warriors.

The Tetons were greatly impressed by the bravery of these white men. The story of their escape spread rapidly among the Indians earning Lewis and Clark the respect of many tribes along the river.

Autumn brought relief from the mosquitoes that had plagued the men since they began their journey. The weather was becoming much cooler now. Some mornings there was ice along the edges of the river. The cold water caused a new problem for the travelers. Some of the men began to suffer from rheumatism. Clark developed this painful condition in his neck and it became almost impossible for him to turn his head.

Large herds of buffalo were seen crossing from the east bank of the river to the west bank. They were followed by Indians seeking to provide a winter supply of meat for their families. One day the captains watched as these hunters killed over 40 of the huge animals.

Two weeks after their incident with the Teton Sioux, Lewis and Clark arrived in an Arikara village. These Indians had already heard about the bravery of the white men. They assured the captains that they had only peaceful intentions and would not try to interfere with the expedition in any way.

While in the camp, York decided to make friends by entertaining the children. He performed feats of strength that delighted the entire village. As the journey progressed, York proved himself to be as intelligent as he was strong. Lewis and Clark found him to be very helpful in making friends with the Native Americans.

Chapter 3

Winter at Fort Mandan

Winter was on the way and the captains knew they needed to find a place to camp. Deep snow and freezing temperatures would soon make travel impossible. Lewis and Clark met two traders who asked to join the expedition for a time. The newcomers told the captains about a large Mandan village not far ahead. Since the Mandans were generally considered friendly to white men, Lewis and Clark thought that perhaps this would be a good place to stop for the winter.

The captains chose a spot about two miles from the Mandan village to build their winter quarters. The area had plenty of timber and enough game to supply their needs.

Since the expedition would remain in this place for almost six months, they needed to build a sturdy, wooden shelter. It was already November and time was short before the snows of winter would cover the ground. The men immediately set to work in order to be finished on time.

They named their new home Fort Mandan. It was a triangular-shaped structure made of logs. Two sides contained large rooms where the men of the expedition lived. The living areas were connected at one end by a look-out tower where a twenty-four hour watch was posted. The third side of the triangle faced the river. It was a wall of upright logs that completed the enclosure and provided protection.

The winters of North Dakota are usually very cold but the winter of 1804–05 was especially severe. The temperature was often below zero for days at a time. Once it dropped to forty-five below. Clark's rheumatism became so painful at times he found it even difficult to eat. However, he never allowed his discomfort to interfere with his work. He continued to draw his maps and complete his journal entries.

The men found it difficult to remain outside for long periods of time. Guards were changed often. They needed a chance to warm themselves beside the fires that were kept blazing inside the fort. Despite this, frostbite was a common occurance.

Hunters who set out from Fort Mandan suffered greatly from the cold. They were often gone for days at a time searching for game on the snow-covered prairie.

While freezing temperatures paralized almost everything outside, the fort was filled with activity inside its protective walls. There was wood to be cut, equipment to be repaired, tools to be made, and trading to be done with the Indians. The captains worked to update their maps and journals. They cleaned and labeled specimens of plants and animals they had collected. Then they packed them to be sent back to St. Louis in the spring. Lewis and Clark made a study of Native American culture in the Mandan village. The captains also spent a great deal of time gathering information from the Indians about the land further west. They learned about mountain passes, waterfalls, rivers, and other landmarks they would encounter in their travels.

During their council meetings with the Indian tribes, Lewis and Clark always told about the "White Father" in Washington who now owned all this land. They said he wanted all Native Americans to live in peace with each

Mandan Chief

other and with the white men. They also expressed Jefferson's desire to begin trading with those who accepted his offer of peace.

Activity at Fort Mandan continued into the evening. This was the time for socializing and relaxing after the day's work. There was dancing almost every night. One of the men, Pierre Cruzat, had brought his fiddle. The Indians enjoyed watching the white men dance to the music of the strange new instrument. They also enjoyed demonstrating their own dances for the Corps of Discovery. The rooms of the fort were filled with music, laughter, and conversation in several different languages.

Lewis and Clark were eager to locate people who could provide information to help them with the next part of their journey. Once they left Fort Mandan, they would have no maps or other documents to use in planning their route. They needed to hire local guides and interpreters.

Toussaint Charbonneau was one of the new men employed by Lewis and Clark. Charbonneau was a French-Canadian trapper who had been serving as an interpreter for traders and Indians in the area. He arrived at Fort Mandan with his three Indian wives and young son. The child was about two years old and also named Toussaint.

Two of Charbonneau's wives were young Shoshoni girls. One of them was about eighteen years old and the other about sixteen. The older girl, Otter Woman, was the mother of little Toussaint. The younger girl was Sacajawea.

It is indicated in the journals that Charbonneau was not well liked or respected by Lewis and Clark. The short, 200 pound trapper was given to bragging, incompetence, and wanting things his own way. It is thought that perhaps he kept his job because the captains recognized the abilities of Sacajawea and wanted to keep her with the expedition.

The captains knew that they would have to locate Indians and purchase horses before they could cross the Rocky Mountains. When they learned that the tribe they would most likely deal with was the Shoshoni tribe, Lewis and Clark became interested in the interpretive abilities of Charbonneau's young wives.

The reason Otter Woman was not considered is unknown. Perhaps she was in poor health or too shy to make a good interpreter. Whatever the reason, the attention of the captains centered on the younger Shoshoni girl.

At first, Lewis thought that Sacajawea was also unfit for the long journey. While at Fort Mandan, she gave birth to her first child, a boy, named Jean Baptiste. The infant was affectionately known as Pomp by members of the expedition. Lewis thought that a young mother with her new-born baby would find the long days of travel in the wilderness far too difficult. Clark explained that the child would be no trouble. Sacajawea was young and strong and could carry the baby safely on her back in a cradleboard. He added that while Charbonneau spoke Minnetaree and some other tribal languages, only Sacajawea spoke Shoshoni. The benefits of taking her along far outweighed the chances of any problems she might cause. Lewis agreed with his partner and Sacajawea became a member of the Corps of Discovery.

Sacajawea has become a famous person in United States history. The idea of a young Indian girl taking part in an exciting adventure such as the Lewis and Clark Expedition provides an excellent topic for storytelling. However, putting the fictional character aside, the real Sacajawea remains as a remarkable woman who made a very real contribution to the Corps of Discovery. Though she was not the guide as some stories claim, she did have importance as an interpreter. She also helped supplement the diet of the men by locating edible roots, berries, and other foods which were a welcome addition to the meat brought in by the hunters. Her presence was the cause of extreme good fortune when the captains located her own band of Shoshoni Indians. Perhaps most important was Sacajawea's role as a symbol of peace. Indians never took women and children into battle. Therefore, when the tribes saw the young mother and her baby, they knew at once that the white men were peaceful. Perhaps this is one reason why the expedition was able to avoid conflicts and to develop good relationships with the tribes they met.

The Shoshonis had no written language. Therefore, little is known about Sacajawea's childhood in the Oregon Country. However, there are some popular accounts which often appear in biographies and retellings of the events in the expedition. Perhaps these have enough basis in fact to give us some insight into the character and background of this outstanding woman.

Toussaint Charbonneau was hired as an interpreter.

Shoshoni children were not given names until something special happened in their lives. They could be named at any time from birth to young adulthood. It is not known if Sacajawea had a childhood name. Lewis and Clark thought that "Sacajawea" was an Indian name probably given her by a plains tribe. The only reference to the possible meaning of "Sacajawea" is in a journal entry dated May 20, 1805. It describes the naming of a branch of the Muscleshell River. It was called Birdwoman's River after the young interpreter. Charbonneau called her Jenny. But, because of his French-Canadian accent, it sounded like "Janey." Therefore, Janey was the nickname by which members of the expedition knew her.

According to some accounts, Sacajawea's father was a leader of the Lemhi Shoshoni. Cameahwait, a close family member, also became a prominent tribal leader. It is not known whether Cameahwait was Sacajawea's brother or her cousin. The Shoshoni language did not provide words to distinguish these family relationships. Children commonly referred to all closely related adults as "mother" or "father" and all closely related youngsters as "brother" or "sister."

The Shoshonis were a proud tribe. They called themselves The People. They believed that they were favored by the Great Spirit and taught their children that being Shoshoni was a great honor.

Having large families was important to the Shoshonis. Everyone worked together and shared what they had. Different bands and families were united through marriage. This gave security and protection to The People who were often in danger of attack from other more war-like tribes. These marriages were arranged by parents when their children were still very young. Sacajawea was promised to the son of a Lemhi warrior when she was still a baby. Her father probably received several fine horses in exchange for the promise of marriage.

The Shoshoni tribe did not farm the land. They considered it foolish to spend one's time planting and caring for crops that nature already produced. This idea appeared to be a good one during years when enough rain fell on their semi-arid land to produce the food they needed. However, some years water was scarce and the soil was too dry to support much vegetation. At these times, the Shoshonis were often hungry. They found it impossible to store enough food for the winter and spring sometimes found them near starvation.

The Minnetarees, fierce warriors who lived to the east of the Shoshonis, often raided neighboring tribes for horses, slaves, and anything else of value they might find. The Minnetarees were farmers and had enough food to keep themselves strong and fit year around. They knew that the Shoshonis were often weakened by hunger in the spring and so chose that time of year to make their raids on the village.

One such attack occurred when Sacajawea was about nine years old. Her parents were killed and she was taken prisoner.

Sacajawea was forced to become a slave of the Minnetarees. She found life in their large village very different from that of her own people. Instead of tepees, the Minnetarees lived in permanent, dome-shaped homes made of earth. Some of these buildings were large enough to stable horses inside. Because these Indians produced their own crops, they did not have to constantly move about following game and searching for food in the manner of the Shoshoni.

Each year, fur trappers, traders, and Indians held a special meeting called a rendezvous. They gathered to exchange goods, gamble, and celebrate. The Minnetarees took Sacajawea to this event and traded her to the Mandans.

When Sacajawea was about 13 years old, Toussaint Char-

Sacajawea was taken prisoner.

bonneau won her while gambling with a Mandan warrior. He took her as his third wife. At the time, Charbonneau was 43 years old. The oldest of his wives was about 16. Charbonneau liked his other wives better than Sacajawea because they obeyed him. When Sacajawea did not, he sometimes beat her with a stick.

Sacajawea was delighted to be traveling with the Corps of Discovery. The expedition would take her back to the land of

The People. After all she had been through, she was going home at last!

Captain Clark's red hair impressed Sacajawea. She had never seen hair that color before. She gave him the nickname, "Chief Red Hair." Lewis also acquired a nickname from the Indians. He came to be known as "Long Knife" because of the military saber he sometimes wore.

Spring finally arrived and the Corps of Discovery prepared to leave Fort Mandan. The men began repairing their pirogues for the journey. Since the river became narrower beyond the fort, the captains decided to send their large keelboat, the Discovery, back to St. Louis. They loaded it with all the records and specimens they had collected. They included pressed plants, animal hides, mineral samples, and Indian artifacts. They also sent some live specimens such as prairie dogs, magpies, and prairie grouse. When the Discovery arrived in St. Louis on May 20, President Jefferson was delighted with the progress of his expedition.

The captains had directed the construction of six dugout canoes to replace the keelboat. These were completed about the same time the Discovery set sail for St. Louis. As soon as the ship departed, the remaining 33 members of the expedition left Fort Mandan to continue their exploration.

Chapter 4
Challenging the Missouri

The land Lewis and Clark now entered was an unexplored wilderness. The members of the Corps of Discovery must have felt a variety of emotions as they departed from Fort Mandan: pride, curiosity, excitement, relief that winter was over, and regret at leaving new friends behind. These feelings were undoubtedly mixed with a certain amount of fear and uneasiness. Lewis expressed this uncertainty when he wrote concerning the journey: " . . . the good or evil it had in store for us was for experiment yet to determine."

Shortly after their departure, Clark vaccinated all the members of the expedition against smallpox. Sacajawea was amazed at the power of these white men. Imagine preventing such a terrible sickness with just one little scratch!

The boats averaged about 20 miles a day traveling up the Missouri River. The men saw large numbers of deer and elk. Lewis often walked along the shore to study the plants and animals. Clark stayed on board to map the land and the river.

By the end of April, they had reached the mouth of the Yellowstone River. Lewis and Drewyer studied the area carefully. They decided that this would make an ideal place for a trading post. It was the meeting place of two important waterways and the rich supply of beaver made it extremely attractive to trappers. The men were correct and twenty-four years later the area became the site of Fort Union.

In addition to knowledge of the land, each day the captains gathered more information about the animal life in the west. Grizzly bears were the most fearsome animals encountered by Lewis and Clark. The Mandans said they never hunted these "yellow bears" without war paint and all the other preparations for battle. Their legends claimed that no single weapon was strong enough to fight this deadly creature. To kill one grizzly was equal to killing two human enemies. Wearing ornaments made from bear claws was a sign of great bravery.

The captains were eager to learn for themselves if these stories were true. On April 28, as Lewis and Drewyer walked along the shore, they encountered two grizzly bears. The

Grizzly bears were the most fearsome animals encountered by Lewis and Clark.

men opened fire and wounded both animals. One of the bears charged at Lewis while the other bear escaped. It chased the captain for 70 or 80 yards. Fortunately, the grizzly was wounded so severely its strength soon gave out. Lewis was able to reload his rifle and kill it. That night, Lewis wrote in his journal:

> The Indians may well fear this animal, equipped as they generally are with their bows and arrows . . . but in the hands of skillful riflemen, they are by no means as formidable or dangerous as they have been presented.

The captain's attitude was soon to change. On May 14, the men in two of the canoes discovered a large grizzly resting on the bank of the river. Six of the best hunters went ashore and crept to within 40 paces of the animal. Four of them opened fire and each managed a direct hit. The huge animal seemed to ignore its wounds. Baring its fangs, the grizzly leaped to its feet and ran directly at the men. The two hunters who had not shot their rifles both fired. One bullet only grazed the bear but the other broke its shoulder. The new injury only momentarily slowed the furious beast. It continued its charge and forced the hunters to retreat to the river. Two of the men escaped in a canoe. The remaining four hid among some willow trees and frantically began to reload and fire their rifles. They were still unable to kill the animal. Their shots only served to draw its attention to their hiding places. The attack of the grizzly was so violent that two of the men dropped their guns and ammunition and dove into the river. The enraged animal plunged in only a few feet behind them. One of the men on shore took careful aim and fired one last time. He killed the bear seconds before it would have reached his helpless companions.

After this narrow escape, Lewis and the others developed a healthy respect for the ferocious grizzlies. The captain agreed with the Indians and wrote "I ... had rather fight two Indians than one bear."

On May 14, another near disaster occurred. Charbonneau had been spending most of his time cooking for the expedition. He thought that he should have a more important job and bragged that he could steer a pirogue as well as anyone. Actually, Charbonneau had no experience and very little ability to perform this important task. The pirogue contained Cruzat, Sacajawea, Pomp, and some of the most valuable supplies and equipment of the expedition. A storm was approaching as Charbonneau took hold of the rudder. The winds rapidly increased and he soon lost control of the boat. Lewis and Clark, who were walking along the shore, shouted instructions but could not be heard above the storm. Huge waves pushed the pirogue sideways and the boat began to fill with water. Charbonneau was terrified. Sacajawea saw many important things being washed overboard. She quickly be-

Charbonneau made a disastrous attempt to steer the pirogue.

gan to retrieve as many as she could. Lewis said she "caught and preserved most of the light articles ... " Despite Charbonneau's ineffectiveness, the explorers managed to save the pirogue. Captain Clark expressed his gratitude to Sacajawea for her quick thinking. Lewis said he could not think of this incident "but with the utmost trepidation and horror."

By late May, Lewis and Clark were in high country as they approached the Rocky Mountains. They first saw these snow-covered peaks on May 26. The captains realized they would encounter increasing hardships as they crossed the steep mountain passes.

It was still very cold in the high elevations through which they traveled. Ice lined the edges of the river. The men had worn out their woolen clothes and were now wearing deerskin clothing and moccasins. These were stiff and heavy because there had not been time to tan the leather properly. The garments were too hot for summer and not warm enough for winter.

The Missouri was becoming a cold mountain river. The banks were slippery with mud and often crumbled causing large chunks of earth to be washed away by the swift current. The river contained many jagged rocks that threatened to pierce the sides of the pirogues and canoes. The wind often became strong enough to force the boats onto the rocks. At those times it became impossible for the men to steer a safe course by rowing. They had to tow their crafts through the narrow channel of the river. The men used ropes made from slender strips of elk hide. Since the ropes were constantly wet and exposed to the weather, they quickly became rotten and were easily broken. When a rope snapped, the men lost control of the boat which was then in danger of being smashed on the rocks.

Towing was difficult, unpleasant work. At times the men waded in icy water up to their armpits for long periods of time. The mud was so sticky they could not wear moccasins. Their unprotected feet were cut and bruised as they walked over sharp rock fragments on the river bottom. Yet, even under these painful conditions, the captains received no complaints.

One night, as the exhausted men slept in their camp beside the river, a large bull buffalo swam toward them from the opposite shore. The animal clambered over the top of a pirogue and charged up the bank. Its sharp hooves came within inches of the sleeping men's heads before a startled sentry sounded the alarm. More men were nearly trampled as the buffalo headed directly toward the tents of Lewis and Clark. Lewis' dog, Scannon, awoke and began barking wildly. This frightened the buffalo away from camp before anyone was injured.

Many of the men did not realize at first what had happened. They had been awakened from a sound sleep by

Scannon frightened a buffalo away from the camp.

shouting, barking, running feet, and general chaos around them. They panicked, grabbed their guns, and were prepared to fight before the captains managed to stop the uproar and explain their narrow escape from the buffalo. Fortunately, there was little damage from this incident. The pirogue needed a few repairs, York's rifle had been trampled, and everyone lost a night's sleep. The men were learning to expect almost anything as they continued their journey to the Pacific.

In June, the Corps of Discovery came to a fork in the river. One branch went north and another branch went south. Indians had told Lewis and Clark that they would pass a huge waterfall on their journey. Beyond, lay the Rocky Mountains and the Continental Divide. Uncertain which route led to the falls, Lewis took some men and explored the north fork of the river. Clark explored the south fork. When the captains returned to their camp, Lewis reported the main part of the Missouri went south. He named the northern branch Marias River.

Travel on the river now became extremely difficult and the captains decided to lighten their cargo as much as possible. They prepared to leave the larger of their two pirogues and some of their extra supplies concealed beside the river until their return to St. Louis. They could use the men from this pirogue to strengthen the crews of the remaining vessels. Lewis and Clark took the pirogue to the middle of a small island at the entrance of Marias River. They tied the boat securely to some trees to prevent its being washed away by floods. Then they carefully covered it with brush to hide it from thieves and protect it from the weather.

Extra supplies and equipment could be safely left behind in a cache. Preparation of the storage area was assigned to Pierre Cruzat who had done this job many times before. Cruzat chose a place near the south branch of the river. He carefully removed a circle of sod about 20 inches in diameter. Then he dug down six or seven feet to create an underground storage place. He made the hole increasingly wider as he worked so the finished opening was shaped like a kettle. Cruzat threw the earth he removed into the river to conceal any evidence of his digging in the area. He built a platform of twigs in the bottom of the pit. This made the floor of the cache which he then covered with an elk skin. This would keep the stored articles dry. He also wrapped the supplies themselves in animal skins to help seal out moisture. Once this was done, he placed the bundles neatly in the cache adding more twigs along the walls for insulation. When he had deposited the last article, Cruzat put one more hide on top and filled the remainder of the hole with earth. He replaced the sod and throughly removed all traces of his presence from the area. When properly constructed and concealed, a cache such as this could safely store supplies for several years.

On June 10, as the captains prepared to explore the area around the Great Falls of the Missouri, Sacajawea suddenly became ill. Both captains were worried and Clark decided to stay in camp and care for her. However, despite his efforts, the Indian woman's pain and fever increased.

When the expedition moved on, Sacajawea was placed in the back of the pirogue where a canopy could protect her from the sun. By June 14, the captains considered her condition to be dangerous and were afraid she would die. They were also concerned about little Pomp who would find it difficult to survive without the care of his mother. The expedition itself would also suffer from the loss of Sacajawea. Dealing with the Shoshoni Indians would become much more complicated.

The captains tried every cure they knew but still Sacajawea's condition became worse. Finally she became so sick

Lewis' Air Gun

An interesting item taken on the expedition was Lewis' air gun. This experimental weapon fired a .28-caliber bullet that lacked force but could kill at short distances. The gun was fired using compressed air which was stored in a removable metal ball. With 300 strokes of the air pump, the gun could be fired 15 or 16 times. The Indians thought there was great magic in a gun that could be fired without powder. Lewis encouraged this belief because it made his men appear more powerful and impressive to the Native Americans. He carried it throughout the expedition and often demonstrated it at council meetings.

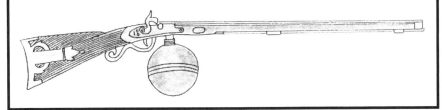

she fell into a deep depression and refused to take any medicine at all. Charbonneau was asked to persuade his wife to accept help. His efforts were successful but the care failed to produce results.

By June 16, Sacajawea's pulse was weak and irregular. The captains had almost given up hope for her recovery. Then the Corps of Discovery arrived at a small mineral spring. Lewis remembered the curative powers of a similar spring back home. He decided to give the water a try. In addition to her regular medicine, Lewis told Sacajawea to drink only from the spring. The expedition remained camped in the area to see if the new treatment would be successful. Within a short time, the Indian woman's health began to return. She accepted some soup made with buffalo meat and began to regain her strength.

Charbonneau now decided that he should be the one to provide food for his wife. He foolishly gave Sacajawea some raw apples and dried fish. Immediately, her illness returned and the expedition was delayed again until she had recovered a second time.

Chapter 5

The Great Falls

Lewis described the Great Falls of the Missouri as "...the grandest sight I ever beheld." He found them exactly as the Indians as had described them. There were a series of five falls. The largest was almost 90 feet high. Lewis devoted a lengthy entry in his journal to a description of the water cascading over the falls to end in "...perfect white foam which assumes a thousand forms in a moment."

The spectacle that inspired such beautiful description soon instilled quite different emotions in the men of the expedition. Traveling around the thundering waterfalls became one of the most difficult parts of the entire journey.

After exploring the river for a distance ahead of them, the captains decided it would be impossible to use the remaining pirogue beyond the falls. They decided to conceal it beside the river. They also dug caches to store the remainder of their extra baggage.

The portage around the falls was 18 miles long. Several trips were needed to transport all the canoes, equipment, and supplies. The men made wooden wheels for their canoes. They used sections of the pirogue's mast for axles. In this way, the boats were transformed into wagons which could be pushed and pulled around the roaring waterfalls.

The Corps of Discovery portaged around the Great Falls of the Missouri River.

The route was extremely difficult. The men pushed their canoes uphill in the midsummer heat. The ground was covered with prickly-pear cactus that stabbed their feet even through double- soled moccasins. Sudden, violent storms often turned the clay soil into a sticky glue that made walking almost impossible. Lewis recorded many hail storms in his journal. He measured hailstones that were seven inches around.

The men were also endangered by grizzly bears. One man saw two of these animals near the river. When he attempted to get a shot at them, he suddenly stumbled upon a third bear. This grizzly attacked him. The frightened explorer ran and fell down a steep bank of the river. He cut his hand, bruised his knees, and bent his gun. Fortunately, the bank concealed him from the enraged bear and he was able to escape. The grizzlies became so troublesome the captains decided that no one should be sent into the brush alone on any errand. They instructed their men to always work in pairs for added protection.

On June 29, Clark, Sacajawea, Pomp, and Charbonneau made a trip to view the falls. As they neared their destination, Clark noticed that a storm was approaching. He looked for shelter and saw a deep ravine nearby with overhanging rocks. He thought this would be a good place to stay dry and wait out the storm.

Thunder echoed across the mountains followed by a heavy rainfall. The wind whipped the rain into their faces making it difficult to see. The party hurried to the ravine for protection from the weather.

As the violent rainstorm continued, the ravine began to fill with water. Clark realized they had chosen a poor place to take shelter. The water rapidly grew deeper and was soon up to the captain's waist.

Clark immediately ordered the others to begin the climb to safety. Charbonneau managed to maintain a grip on the slippery rock wall of the ravine and pull himself up to a higher ledge. The captain took Pomp from Sacawajea and handed him up to his father. Next, he boosted the Indian woman toward the ledge telling her terrified husband to take her hand and pull her up. Charbonneau was by now so frightened he did not respond to the command. He sat motionless clinging to his child and watching the water rise higher and higher. Clark frantically managed to push Sacajawea onto the ledge and scramble to safety himself. Just as he did so, a huge wall of water crashed through the ravine below them. They had narrowly escaped death in the flash flood.

Sacajawea was so wet and cold Clark was afraid her recent illness might reoccur. All of Pomp's things: his cradleboard, bedding, and clothing, had been lost in the flood. Clark had also lost a compass which was very important to him in his work. The water had risen to at least 15 feet so it was impossible to return and search for the missing items.

When the little group of explorers reached the top of the ravine, they were met by Ben York who had been searching for his master and the others. York helped them back to their camp where they discovered that no one had escaped the fury of the storm. Many of the men had been knocked down by strong winds and left bruised and bleeding by the huge hailstones. All of them were wet and miserable as they looked for dry clothing in their scattered baggage.

The day after the storm, the captains returned to the ravine. They were able to find the lost compass which had nearly been buried in the mud. The ravine itself was almost completely filled with rocks carried in by the flash flood. Clark shuddered at the realization that he and his compan-

Captain Clark and his companions narrowly escaped death in a flash flood.

ions would surely have been killed if they had not managed to reach the ledge.

When they had recovered from the storm, the explorers continued their portage around the falls. Lewis had brought a portable boat frame which he had designed and named the Experiment. He thought this 44-pound craft could easily be transported around the falls. After the portage, the men could assemble the iron framework and cover it with bark to produce a canoe. The Experiment could then replace the larger boats which had been left behind. After reaching the Great Falls, Lewis discovered that no suitable bark was available. He decided to substitute buffalo hides which seemed to work very well for the Indians who used them as coverings for their bullboats. The captain was very disappointed when the hides also proved unsatisfactory for covering a boat as large as the Experiment. One hide was not big enough and the men had to stitch several together. They found it impossible to make the seams watertight. The hides shrank, crevices opened, and the boat sank. Lewis was convinced that his idea would have worked if the hair had been left on the hides. He saw no shrinking or leaking in parts of the boat where the hair had not been removed. He needed new hides that were tanned with the hair still on them. However, since there were no buffalo in the area or time to hunt for them, Lewis sadly left his "favorite boat" behind. The men were required to build two dugout canoes to replace the Experiment.

By July 15, 1805, the portage around the Great Falls was completed. The expedition now traveled in eight canoes up the Missouri. The canoes were so heavily loaded with supplies that Lewis and some of the men were forced to walk along the shore.

Chapter 6

Return to the Land of The People

On July 19, the Corps of Discovery reached a place where they had a magnificent view of the mountains and valleys before them. They named this area the Gates of the Rocky Mountains.

The captains were anxious to make contact with the Shoshoni Indians. They knew they must cross the mountains before winter blocked the passes and made travel impossible. They needed to locate the Indians and purchase horses to carry them on this part of their journey.

Lewis and Clark were afraid that their hunters might frighten the Indians away with their daily rifle fire. They thought the Shoshonis might hear the shots and think they were about to be attacked by their enemies. The captains decided that a small group of men should travel up the river on foot ahead of the main expedition. They would attempt to meet the Indians before they could be alarmed by the sight or sound of the entire Corps of Discovery. It was important to establish a friendly relationship with the Shoshonis as soon as possible. Clark volunteered to lead this group taking Field, Potts, and York with him.

Walking was extremely difficult for Clark and his men. Prickly- pear and other sharp thorns pierced their moccasins and leggings making each step painful. Scannon needed the exercise of running along the shore but suffered a great deal and was "constantly biting and scratching himself as if in a rack of pain."

On July 22, Sacajawea recognized the area they were traveling through. She said the river would soon branch into three parts. Just as she predicted, a few days later the expedition reached a place now known as the Three Forks of the Missouri. After studying each division of the river, the captains decided to take the southwestern fork because it led more directly toward the western mountains. They called this division the Jefferson River. They also named the remaining branches after important governmental officials. The southeast fork became the Gallatin after Secretary of the Treasury, Albert Gallatin. The middle fork became the Madison after Secretary of State, James Madison.

Lewis wrote that on July 28, the expedition camped on the exact spot where Sacajawea's people had been attacked by the Minnetarees. He said when the enemy warriors rode into the camp, the Shoshonis

> ... retreated about three miles up Jefferson's river and concealed themselves in the woods. The Minnetarees pursued, attacked them, killed four men, four women, a number of boys, and made prisoners of all the females and four boys. Sacajawea, our Indian woman, was one of the female prisoners taken at that time ...

Sacajawea seemed to display no emotion at being in this place once again. Lewis thought her attitude was somewhat strange. She seemed content with her new life as a member of the Corps of Discovery. Perhaps she had learned to accept the terrible events that had separated her from The People.

Early in August, the expedition suddenly encountered rapids as they traveled on the river. One canoe overturned drenching its entire cargo including the valuable medicine

Sacajawea recognized the place where she had been captured by the Minnetarees.

box. Several articles were lost and never recovered. Lewis most regretted the loss of "a shot pouch and horn and all the implements for one rifle."

Later that same day the men lost control of two other canoes in the treacherous white water of the Jefferson River. One of the dugouts swung abruptly in the rapids throwing a man into the rushing water. The boat then passed directly over him as he fought to reach the surface. Lewis wrote that if the water had been two inches shallower, the swimmer would have been crushed to death beneath the boat.

Sacajawea now recognized a tall rock at a distance that her people called Beaverhead Rock. She told the captains that they were not far from the summer home of The People. If they continued to follow the Jefferson River, they should soon make contact with the Shoshonis. This information gave encouragement to the tired men. Battered by the rapids and suffering from the thorns on the shore, they needed to know they would soon find the help they were searching for.

Travel continued to be very difficult. Lewis feared they might discover another waterfall at any time. Even though Sacajawea assured him they would not, the captain continued to worry. It was hard for him to believe they could continue to follow the river through such rugged country without encountering more dangerous rapids or falls. The water was now so shallow in places the canoes had to be dragged over the rocks. The men were forced to walk in the river because of the thick brush along the shore. The slippery rocks caused many of them to fall. Clark suffered from an infected ankle, Charbonneau limped for days, and Drewyer injured his back. The members of the expedition grew more and more impatient to leave the river and continue their journey by land.

On August 11, Lewis took Drewyer, Shields, and McNeal and began to search for Indians. After traveling only about five miles, they became aware of a man on horseback watching them. Lewis wrote:

> ... I discovered from his dress that he was of a different nation from any that we had yet seen and was satisfied of his being a Shoshoni. His arms were a bow and a quiver of arrows, and he was mounted on an elegant horse without a saddle, and a small string which was attached as a bridle.

Captain Lewis removed the blanket from his pack. He unfolded it and waved it over his head and back to the ground as if he were spreading it out to sit on. He did this three times as a sign of welcome, but the Indian did not move.

Next, Lewis called out, "Tab-ba-bone, tab-ba-bone." He thought this meant "white man" in Shoshoni and would help indicate his friendly intentions. This was a serious mistake. Lewis could have not chosen a worse expression. The word, "tab-ba-bone," actually meant "stranger" which was

Lewis and his men saw a Shoshoni warrior watching them from a distance.

47

almost the same as "enemy" in those times. The Shoshonis had no word for "white man" in their vocabulary. Lewis had asked Sacajawea for a word to use in referring to his people. Since she could think of nothing else and white men were strangers to her people, she told him to use "tab-ba-bone." This greeting only caused the rider to become more suspicious and uneasy.

Lewis ordered his men to remain where they were and not attempt to approach the Indian. Shields, however, did not hear the command and continued to advance. Seeing this, the rider turned his horse, leaped over a creek, and disappeared into the brush. Lewis was very disappointed at the loss of his first opportunity for a friendly meeting with the Shoshonis. He decided to follow the Indian back to the other members of his tribe.

Captain Lewis and his men followed the rider over the Continental Divide at Lemhi Pass. There they encountered another Shoshoni warrior accompanied by two women. They appeared to be watching the white men from a safe distance. Lewis ordered his men to wait and, placing his rifle and pack on the ground, slowly approached the Indians. The women immediately became frightened and ran away. The man appeared to be more curious and sat down to study the newcomers. The captain unfolded a flag that he carried and waved it as a sign of friendship. He also shouted the word, "tab- ba-bone," which he still thought meant "white man." All at once, the warrior seemed to become alarmed. Leaping to his feet, he also fled leaving Lewis to wonder what mistake he continued to make with these people.

There was nothing left to do but regroup and try again. The next opportunity arrived sooner than any of the men expected. They had only traveled about a mile further when they discovered another small group of Indians. This time they met an old woman and two young girls looking for food in a ravine. The youngest girl fled immediately when she saw the strangers. The others also became alarmed but seemed to think the intruders were already too close for them to escape capture. They sat down and bowed their heads in a jesture of submission. The women were prepared to face death bravely according to the teachings of their people.

Once again the captain laid aside his gun and approached the Shoshonis. He took the old woman by the hand and gently lifted her to her feet. Then Lewis pulled up his shirt sleeve to display his untanned arm. In this way he hoped to show he was a white man and not a member of an enemy tribe. The explorers gave the women gifts of friendship. They presented them with beads, awls, mirrors, and face paint. Lewis told Drewyer to use sign language and ask the old woman to call back the girl who had run away. He was afraid she would alarm her people before he had a chance to make peaceful contact with them. The old woman agreed and the young girl timidly returned. She was also given presents by the explorers. Lewis dabbed vermillion, a red paint, on the women's cheeks. Sacajawea had told him this was a sign of peace. He used sign language to indicate he wanted them to lead the way to their camp. The women were calmer now and no longer feared the white men. They agreed to take the strangers to their people.

The little group had traveled only about two miles when a band of 60 armed warriors charged toward them on horseback. The first Indians Lewis encountered had returned home to spread the alarm. The Shoshonis thought they were about to be attacked by their old enemies, the Minnetarees. They had immediately prepared for battle by arming themselves with bows, arrows, shields, and a few old guns obtained from neighboring tribes.

Realizing the danger to their new friends, the three

women ran to the warriors holding up their presents to show that the strangers were peaceful.

The Indian leader was relieved to know his people were safe from attack. He welcomed the white men and embraced them according to Shoshoni custom.

The warriors took Lewis and his men back to their village. Everyone was excited and eager to see them. They were the first white men ever to visit this area in present-day Idaho.

The explorers were escorted to a council lodge made of willow branches and leather hides. Before sitting down to smoke the pipe of peace, the Shoshonis took off their moccasins and indicated their guests should do the same. This custom was a sign of friendship and good will. It indicated that anyone at the meeting who was not sincere and truthful should have to walk barefoot forever as a punishment.

In honor of their guests, the Shoshonis celebrated most of the night. Lewis exchanged gifts with them and asked their

Lewis located a group of Shoshoni Indians led by Cameahwait.

help in bringing the rest of his expedition to their village. The captain presented their leader, whose name was Cameahwait, with a Jefferson Peace Medal in appreciation for his hospitality.

Chapter 7
Cameahwait

Lewis was grateful to have finally located the Shoshonis. However, he did not as yet fully understand his incredible good fortune. He had just met the very same group of Indians from which Sacajawea had been taken as a child. The leader, Cameahwait, was a member of her immediate family. This situation no doubt greatly helped the captains in persuading the Indians to part with some of their valuable horses. The reunion of Sacajawea with the remainder of her family would insure feelings of friendship and trust between the men of the expedition and the Shoshoni people.

The morning after their first meeting, the warriors seemed afraid to accompany the white men to their camp. Strangers were usually considered to be enemies and the Indians thought Lewis and his men might be leading them into some kind of a trap. Even though they seemed harmless, perhaps these three visitors were allies of the Minnetarees. A large war party could be waiting just outside the village. The unsuspecting Shoshonis could be easily ambushed once they left the safety of their camp.

Lewis assured Cameahwait of his honorable intentions and repeated his request for help in transporting his men and supplies to the Indian village. He said there must be at least a few warriors brave enough to risk leaving the camp. It was a sad thing to see an entire Shoshoni band so frightened by three peaceful strangers.

Cameahwait wanted to prove his bravery. He agreed to accompany Lewis and challenged the others to do the same. At first, only a few agreed to go. Soon, however, more men and even some women joined the group.

The Indians had been short of food for many days. Hunting was difficult using only bows and arrows. Lewis and his men shot several deer and antelope on the way to meet Clark and the rest of the expedition. This food helped encourage the Shoshonis to remain with the white men. Lewis aroused the Indians' curiosity by telling them they would soon meet a Shoshoni girl who had been captured by the Minnetarees and see a man who was black with short, curly hair. The Indians, who were still unaccustomed to white skin, found it almost impossible to accept the idea of black skin and curly hair. They were eager to see if this could be true. Full stom-

Sacajawea   **Cameahwait**

achs and active imaginations helped Cameahwait's people push the fear of treachery and ambush from their minds.

On August 17, an Indian scout spotted Clark and the Corps of Discovery traveling on the river a short distance away. The Shoshonis were excited and happy to meet the rest of Lewis' companions. They were also relieved that their trust in the captain had not been misplaced.

Captain Clark, Charbonneau, and Sacajawea were the first to reach Lewis and the others. One of the Indian women seemed fascinated by Sacajawea. After gazing at her for some time, the woman ran to the interpreter's wife and threw her arms around her. Only then did Sacajawea recognize her friend who had also been captured by the Minnetarees. While Sacajawea had been unable to escape, her friend had managed to slip away and return home. Both women were overjoyed to see each other again.

This was to be a day of many reunions for Sacajawea. The women's excited laughter and conversation soon attracted the attention of Cameahwait. Moving closer, he was astonished to discover Sacajawea had returned home unharmed. Lewis commented that "the meeting of those people was really affecting."

This special day was not, however, without its touch of sadness. After their first joyful meeting, Sacajawea asked Cameahwait about the rest of their family. He sadly told her they were all dead except for himself and two other male relatives. One of these was a small boy who the captains believed was the son of Sacajawea's older sister. According to Shoshoni custom, the interpreter's wife now assumed responsibility for the young child. Before continuing the journey with Lewis and Clark, she entrusted his care to Cameahwait so he could remain and be raised in the Oregon Country.

A council meeting was held. Lewis and Clark were anxious to begin trading for horses as soon as possible. Captain

Clark had discovered the river ahead was too dangerous for travel by canoe. Horses were now the only possible means of transportation.

Using Sacajawea as interpreter, the captains told Cameahwait and his people they needed horses and guides to cross the mountains. They explained the purpose of their mission and how it would benefit the Shoshonis in the future. They said that once they had successfully completed their exploration, traders would follow bringing many wonderful things. Guns would then be available for hunting and protection.

After hearing this, the Indians became more interested and expressed their desire to cooperate. The captains said the success of their expedition was now in the hands of Cameahwait's people. The white men needed horses immediately to cross the mountains before winter blocked their passage. Without horses, the white men would end their journey and return home. Traders would never bring guns to the Shoshonis.

Cameahwait liked the white men and wanted them to stay awhile. Clark described him as "... a man of influence, sense, and easy and reserved manners. Appears to possess a great deal of sincerity."

Lewis and Clark had difficulty buying enough horses to transport all their men and supplies. The Indians were about to leave on their annual buffalo hunt and had few horses to spare. The captains managed to purchase only 29 of these animals. Clark wrote that they were generally of poor quality. They were too young or too old and broken down. Many of them were not accustomed to carrying packs and were difficult to handle.

By the end of August the Lewis and Clark Expedition was prepared to leave the Shoshoni camp. The men had dug a cache to store the things they did not need or could not take with them. They had made leather sacks to carry their gear and supplies. They had also constructed saddles for their horses using wood from empty boxes and canoe oars. Cameahwait recommended that they ask an old warrior named Toby to become their guide across the Rocky Mountains. He knew more about the land north of the river than anyone else in the village. Old Toby agreed to accompany the white men on their journey and took his son along to help.

Chapter 8
Lolo Pass and Beyond

The Corps of Discovery used the Lolo Trail to cross the rugged Bitterroot Range of the Rocky Mountains. This was the route traveled by the Nez Perce Indians when they set out to hunt buffalo each year. The journey turned out to be one of the greatest ordeals of the entire expedition.

Before reaching the trail, the travelers met a large band of Salish Indians in the valley of the Bitterroot River. These people were also known as Flatheads even though they did not practice the custom of head flattening common in some other tribes. The Salish were also about to begin a buffalo hunt. They had a large number of horses. Clark counted at least 500.

The captains found it very difficult to communicate with these people. Their language was different from any the expedition had encountered so far. Fortunately, the white men discovered a Shoshoni boy living with the Salish. He was able to talk with Sacajawea and act as an interpreter for the Indians.

Clark managed to buy about thirteen horses and exchange several weak animals for stronger ones. The Salish leader warned the white men they would have difficulty finding food on the trail ahead. The captains decided to remain camped an extra day to hunt and graze their horses. Then they would be ready to endure the hardships of the Lolo Trail.

The journey was much more difficult than anyone was prepared for. It had already begun to snow in the mountains. The trail was slippery and treacherous. Huge fallen trees blocked the way completely in some places and the men had to cut their way through. The horses often lost their footing on the steep hillsides. Some of them were crippled when they slipped and fell down the rugged slopes.

Cold, bitter winds drove sleet and snow into the men's faces making it difficult to see the trail ahead. The explorers painfully traveled on with their feet nearly frozen in their moccasins. They were almost out of food but no one would risk leaving the main expedition to hunt. The chance of getting lost in the white wilderness was far too great. When the men finally became ill from starvation, they killed and ate three of their horses. The Indians had said that crossing the Bitterroot Range should take about five days. However, the men with Lewis and Clark suffered for eleven days while completing this terrible part of their journey.

On September 20, the expedition met a small group of Nez Perce Indians. By that time the explorers had traveled over the worst part of the Lolo Trail.

Lewis and Clark believed the Nez Perce were friendly to them from the beginning. However, there are some tribal stories that suggest otherwise. One says that the Indians had considered an attack on the expedition. They viewed the white men as strangers and a possible threat to their safety. The battle was prevented by a Nez Perce woman named Stray Away. Her life had once been saved by a white trapper and she wanted to repay the debt. Since many of the other Nez Perce legends about the expedition have proven to be true when compared with historical records, the story of

Chief Twisted Hair welcomed the Corps of Discovery to his village.

Stray Away may also have a basis in fact. Whether or not this actually happened, the important thing was the friendly reception Lewis and Clark received when they finally arrived in the land of the Nez Perce.

The Indians introduced the captains to their chief whose name was Twisted Hair. They said he was one of the most respected leaders in the area. Clark described him as "a cheerful man with apparent sincerity." The chief invited the white men to stay and rest awhile after their difficult trip over the mountains.

In the village, the starving explorers gorged themselves on salmon and camas root. The large quantity of food was too much of a shock for their empty stomachs. Eating too much too fast made their condition worse instead of better. The members of the expedition became so sick it was almost a week before some of them were able to continue work.

The captains held a council with Twisted Hair and the other important chiefs. They explained their mission and presented gifts of friendship to those present. They asked the Indians to provide them with information about the land ahead. Twisted Hair drew a map of the river beyond his camp on a white elk skin. Three young warriors and two chiefs agreed to become guides and travel with the expedition for a time.

Even though most of the men still suffered from upset stomachs, Lewis and Clark knew they must begin preparations to resume their journey. They learned that travel on the river was once again possible. The expedition would be able to continue down the Clearwater and Snake rivers to the Columbia River.

The explorers branded their horses and arranged to leave them in the care of the Nez Perce. They set up camp along

The captains held a council with Twisted Hair and the other Nez Perce chiefs.

the Clearwater River in a place where large ponderosa pines were available to make dugout canoes. The men were still weak from their recent illness. Therefore, instead of using chisels to hollow out the logs, they chose the easier Indian method of burning away the excess wood. By October 7, they had completed five canoes and were ready to travel again.

Chapter 9
On to the Pacific

The current of the Clearwater River was very swift. Canoes were often upset and damaged as the men attempted to steer a safe course through the rapids. Sometimes the captains decided the river was too dangerous and ordered a portage to calmer water.

The captains were surprised on October 9 to learn that their guides, Old Toby and his son, had mysteriously left the expedition. The two Shoshonis had decided to return home without telling anyone or receiving pay for the work they had done. Lewis and Clark asked the Nez Perce guides to send someone after the pair to bring them back. The chiefs advised against this. They said the Shoshonis realized they could be of no further help this far from their own country. Toby was probably afraid of being robbed on the way home if he carried gifts from the white men. The captains finally agreed that it was best not to interfere with the old man's decision. They allowed the Shoshoni guides to depart in this manner even though they regretted not repaying them for their help.

After a few more days of travel, the expedition arrived at the place where the Clearwater River joins the Snake River. Clark wrote that for the last three weeks his men had eaten almost nothing but fish. They were very tired of this and decided to buy several dogs from the Indians for food. Eating dog meat was a common practice among many tribes and everyone except Clark and Sacajawea enjoyed this change in diet.

On October 16, the expedition reached the Columbia River. Clark noticed many Indians catching and drying salmon. The Indians invited the travelers to stop and share a meal. The women in the village heated rocks and used them to boil water in woven baskets. They cooked the fish in the boiling water and served them on small, woven mats. Clark was amazed at the great quantity of salmon available. While in the village, the captain also noticed that these Indians did not live in tepees. Their woven grass lodges were rectangular in shape and up to 60 feet long.

While on the Columbia River, the Corps of Discovery passed many Indian villages. The Nez Perce guides traveled ahead of the expedition to assure the tribes that the white men were peaceful. Indians often gathered near the shore to watch the strangers pass by in their canoes. Stories about the journey of Lewis and Clark would be told around campfires for many years. It was an exciting event in tribal history.

Despite the efforts of the Nez Perce guides, some Indians remained afraid of the white men. On October 19, Clark and two men traveled ahead of the main group of explorers. They arrived at a small village located where the Umatilla River joins the Columbia River. Clark recorded that the Indians were terrified of the white men and hid in their lodges. He learned they thought the travelers "came from the clouds and were not men." Clark entered one of the lodges carrying his pipe as a sign of peace. Inside he found thirty-two frightened people crying and wringing their hands. Despite reassurance from the captain and his men, the Indians did not calm down completely until the arrival of Sacajawea. Clark wrote that when they saw her, they came outside "and appeared to assume new life. The sight of this Indian woman... [assured] these people of our friendly intentions... no woman ever accompanied a war party in this quarter." The villagers lost their fear of the white men and smoked the pipe of peace with them.

Travel on the Columbia River proved more dangerous than either the Clearwater or the Snake rivers. There were many rapids. One of them was two miles long. It required two hours of exhausting labor to steer the canoes safely through. Other hazards were created by islands, rocks, waterfalls, and the occasional narrowing of the river channel.

On October 23, Lewis and Clark had to portage around Celilo Falls. The Indians used their horses to help carry the expedition's supplies. The canoes had to be lowered from the top of the falls using ropes made from elk skin. During this process, a rope snapped sending one of the canoes hurtling to the river below. Fortunately, it was retrived by the Indians before it could be lost or destroyed in the foaming water at the base of the falls.

The Nez Perce guides said they wanted to return home on October 24. Their people were at war with the tribes in this area and they thought they were in danger. They were also unfamiliar with the languages here and could no longer serve effectively as guides. The captains persuaded them to remain a short while longer. They had learned that the next section of the river was also extremely dangerous and they needed all the help they could get.

The part of the river they now entered was called the Short Narrows. An enormous rock almost completely blocked the channel leaving an opening only about forty-five yards wide. The water was "thrown into whirls and swells" as it boiled through this narrow passage. Since the men were already exhausted and lacked enough strength for a portage, the captains decided to risk taking their canoes through the fierce rapids. Many Indians lined the top of the canyon wall to watch the explorers risk their lives in the turbulent water below. The expedition's best waterman, Pierre Cruzat, led the way. Using all his skill, he safely steered his canoe through the narrow gorge to safety on the other side. The remaining explorers soon followed accompanied by cheers from the Indian spectators.

The canoes had only traveled about a mile further when they were once again stopped by rapids. This time they looked so dangerous the captains ordered all the men who could not swim to go ashore. They would transport the most important baggage by land. The rest of the men took the canoes in pairs through the swirling water. It took the expedition an entire day to travel only six miles on this section of the Columbia.

Some Indians welcomed the explorers into their village at

The explorers risked their lives in the hazardous Short Narrows.

the end of the day. When it was discovered they were members of the tribe feared by the Nez Perce guides, the captains took the opportunity to express Jefferson's wish that all Native Americans live together in peace. Lewis and Clark gave medals and other gifts of friendship to the important men of the village. Cruzat played his violin and the white men danced to the delight of the Indians. By the end of the evening, everyone was in high spirits and the captains had every reason to believe the Nez Perce no longer needed to fear their former enemies.

On October 25, Lewis and Clark said goodby to their Nez Perce guides. Clark wrote they stopped work to smoke "a parting pipe with our two faithful friends, the chiefs who accompanied us from the head of the river."

The journey continued to be difficult as the explorers traveled through the Cascade Mountains. The river contained many rapids. The men had to portage several times. Boats were damaged and had to be repaired.

By November 7, 1805, the Lewis and Clark Expedition was within 15 miles of the Pacific Ocean. Clark excitedly wrote in his journal:

> O the joy! That ocean, the object of all our labors, the reward of all our anxieties. The cheering view exhilarated the spirits of all the party, who were still more delighted on hearing the distant roar of the breakers.

Before the explorers could reach the coast, they still had to cross the broad expanse of water at the mouth of the Columbia River. The members of the Corps of Discovery were the first white men to reach the mouth of the Columbia traveling overland from the east. However, this knowledge gave them little pleasure at first. Problems immediately arose to overshadow the joy of accomplishment.

Clark wrote that the expedition was delayed for several days because "we found the swells or waves so high that we thought it imprudent to proceed."

It rained continuously during this delay causing the men to become "wet and disagreeable." High cliffs along the shore kept the explorers too near the river for them to establish a suitable campsite. The waves tossed the canoes about with such force that several of the travelers became seasick.

By November 12, the expedition had traveled 10 miles further and made camp in a sheltered cove. However, even there, the terrible weather continued to make their lives miserable. Clark listed their situation as "dangerous." He wrote:

> It would be distressing to see our situation—all wet and cold, our bedding also wet . . . our baggage half a mile from us, and canoes at the mercy of the waves . . . one [canoe] got loose last night and was left on a rock a short distance below, without receiving more damage than a split . . .

The captains realized they would never reach the coast by boat. They decided to explore the rest of the distance to the ocean by foot. They were relieved to discover the Pacific was now only a few miles away.

The explorers soon met some Chinook Indians who lived in the area. One of them had a robe made of two sea otter skins. This was the most beautiful fur the captains had ever seen. Both Lewis and Clark attempted to purchase the robe but all their offers were refused. Finally, Clark struck a bargain using a belt of blue beads provided by Sacajawea. Beads of this color were known as "chief beads" and highly prized by many tribes. The captains presented Sacajawea with a blue coat in appreciation for her generosity.

The explorers were eager for news of other white men in the area. They hoped to locate the captain of a trading vessel and obtain a ride home by sea. Lewis and Clark met Indians at the mouth of the Columbia River who wore clothing and carried items they had purchased from white men. One of the warriors even spoke a few words of English. Though these Indians spoke of many visits by American traders, no ships were ever sighted by the expedition. Winter was already upon them. The Corps of Discovery would have to remain camped near the Columbia River and return overland to St. Louis in the spring.

Lewis and Clark asked the coastal tribes about other white men in the area.

Chapter 10
Fort Clatsop

On November 24, the captains held a meeting to decide where to build their winter home. Each member of the expedition was given a chance to speak. The men wanted a place where hunting was good. They also wanted a mild climate and an easy approach for any ship that might travel into the Columbia. Lewis and Clark knew they would need a fresh supply of salt for the return trip. They wanted the camp to be in a convenient location for salt- making. Sacajawea added that she would like a spot where there were plenty of delicious wapato roots for baking.

The expedition finally selected a place south of the Columbia inland from the coast. The men immediately began chopping down trees for logs to build their enclosure. By Christmas Day, 1805, the buildings were almost finished. The stockade was 50 feet square and contained seven small cabins. The captains named it Fort Clatsop after the friendly Clatsop Indians who lived nearby.

On Christmas morning, Lewis and Clark were awakened by gunfire. The men had discharged their rifles in a salute to this special day. They continued their celebration with shouts, cheers, and songs. The captains presented each member of the expedition with a small gift. They gave tobacco to those who smoked and handkerchiefs to the others.

The mood of the celebration soon grew melancholy. The men were accustomed to a large Christmas dinner with all the trimmings. This year, their meal consisted of spoiled elk meat, pounded salmon, and a few roots. The food was almost inedible. The explorers missed their families and friends. The bleak, rainy weather also added to their misery. The cold drizzle outside made everyone grateful for at least one thing—the snug warmth of their new cabins.

The finishing touches were added to Fort Clatsop on December 30. Almost immediately, the captains directed Drewyer to take four men and begin hunting for food. Three other men were sent to establish a camp near the ocean and begin replenishing the expedition's salt supply.

Many Indians visited the fort each day. Though friendly

The Lewis and Clark Expedition spent the winter of 1805-06 at Fort Clatsop near the Pacific Ocean.

with the local tribes, the captains established strict rules to protect the safety of their men and supplies. Guards were posted both day and night. They reported the arrival and departure of all visitors to their commanding officers. The men were ordered to treat all Indians in a respectful manner. However, they had the right to refuse admittance to their private rooms if they wished. The members of the expedition were also allowed to protect themselves if threatened by one of the visitors. Indians who refused to obey the rules inside the fort were forced to leave and could not return until the next day. At sunset each day, Charbonneau and three others were responsible for making sure all visitors left the fort. Indians were not allowed to remain inside at night without special permission from Lewis and Clark. The gates of Fort Clatsop remained closed and locked until sunrise the next morning. The sergeant of the guard kept the key to the supply house. It was his duty to protect the contents and maintain the fires there to keep the food and equipment from freezing. It was also his job to check the canoes every 24 hours to be sure they remained safe and secure. All members of the Corps of Discovery were required to help provide food and everyone except cooks and interpreters must take their turn at guard duty. Anyone caught trading supplies to the Indians without permission could be tried and punished for stealing. By strict enforcement of these rules, the captains helped ensure a peaceful winter on the Pacific coast.

On January 1, 1806, Lewis and Clark again awoke to a salute of rifle fire. Lewis wrote that this was the "only mark of respect given this respected day." Though the food was now somewhat better than it had been on Christmas, the men preferred to think about New Year's Day, 1807 when they would be home again with their loved ones. They promised they would never again take for granted the pleasures provided by the "hand of civilization."

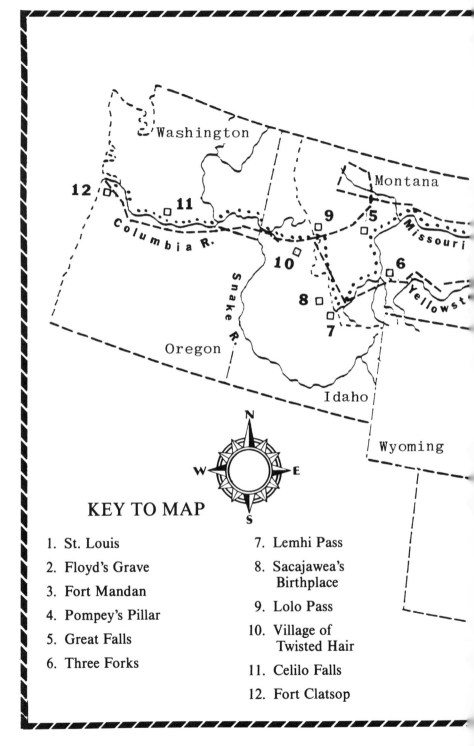

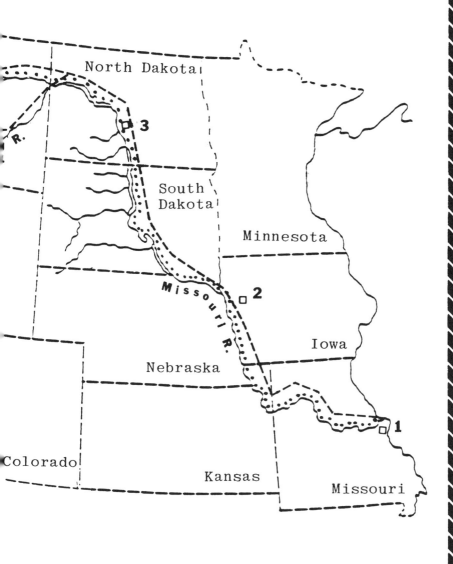

The captains sent two men to check the progress of the salt makers in their camp on the Pacific coast. They returned on January 5 and reported that everything was going well. The workers were able to produce from three quarts to a gallon of salt a day. The men brought back some blubber the Indians had given them. It had been taken from a whale that had died and been washed up on the beach. Clark wrote that, when cooked, the blubber was tender and good to eat. It tasted almost like beaver meat.

Captain Clark decided to take some men and see the whale for himself. He hoped to be able to get more blubber from the carcass. If not, perhaps he could purchase some from the Indians.

Sacajawea wanted to accompany the men to the coast. Clark wrote:

> She observed that she had traveled a long way with us to see the great waters and, now that monstrous fish was also to be seen, she thought it very hard that she could not be permitted to see either.

The captain agreed with Sacajawea and decided to take the Indian woman and her child along.

On the coast, Clark and his men found the salt camp in a good location near wood, salt water, and the fresh water of a nearby river. The men had built several fireplaces where they boiled down sea water to remove the salt.

The captain hired a young local guide and immediately set out to locate the whale. When he found it, he was disappointed to see only the skeleton of the 105-foot animal. The Tillamook Indians had already removed all the blubber from the bones.

Though the Indians possessed large quantities of oil and blubber, Clark was only able to purchase a small amount. The captain was grateful for what he received and wrote:

The coastal tribes lived in wooden longhouses.

... thank Providence for directing the whale to us; and think Him much more kind to us than He was to Jonah, having sent this monster to be swallowed by us, instead of swallowing of us, as Jonah's did.

The Indians encountered by the expedition were generally honest and trustworthy. However, there are exceptions to every rule. One such unfortunate incident occurred on January 8 while Clark and his men were still at the salt making camp.

An Indian invited Private Hugh McNeal to have dinner and spend the evening in his lodge. When McNeal arrived, the man seemed dissatisfied with the meal prepared by his wife. He asked his guest to accompany him to another lodge for something better. Hearing this, the woman became upset and attempted to prevent McNeal from leaving. He ignored her protests and followed her husband from the lodge. Outside, the explorer was startled when another woman he knew suddenly ran toward him screaming and frantically waving her arms. Seeing this, McNeal's host immediately turned and fled from the village. The confused white man soon learned he had narrowly escaped death. The man who invited him to dinner had planned to rob and murder him when they reached the second lodge. Fortunately, the plan had been discovered by the explorer's friend who shouted her warning just in time to prevent the terrible act. The would-be robber managed to escape and never returned to the village.

McNeal immediately reported the incident to Clark who was also visiting the lodge of an Indian family. The captain had heard the scream and hurried outside to investigate. He was greatly relieved to learn that none of his men had been harmed. However, the threat of violence made all of the explorers uneasy and placed them on their guard.

Shortly after the middle of March, the captains began their final preparations to leave Fort Clatsop. The men had made enough salt and gathered enough food for the return journey. They had repaired their clothing, canoes and guns. Since no ships had arrived to take them home, the explorers were eager to begin the long overland trip.

Unknown to the men of the expedition, the Lydia, a trading ship from Boston, had visited the mouth of the Columbia in November, 1805. The captain had been told about Lewis and Clark but was unable to locate them. The Lydia continued to travel along the Pacific coast until August, 1806. By that time, the Corps of Discovery was almost home. The explorers had missed their chance for a return voyage by sea.

Before leaving the coast, Lewis and Clark posted a message in their quarters for any "civilized person" who visited Fort Clatsop after they were gone. They wanted it known that the buildings had been constructed by an American ex-

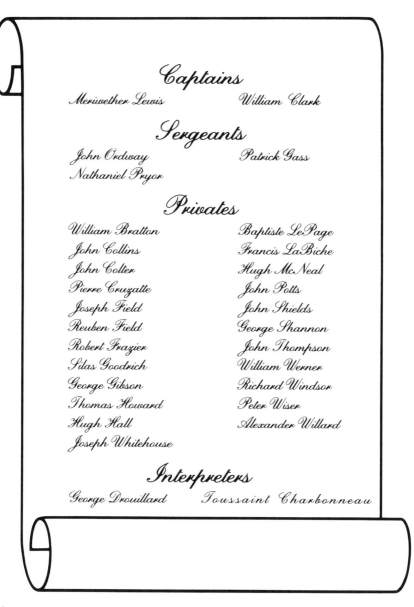

The captains posted a list of the explorers at Fort Clatsop.

pedition sent " . . . to explore the interior of the continent of North America . . . by way of the Missouri and Columbia rivers." The captains included the dates of their arrival and departure from the fort and a list of the members of the Corps of Discovery. Copies of this document were given to several of the coastal tribes. One copy eventually came to the attention of the captain of the Lydia. He carried it to Boston with him to make certain the United States was informed of the success of the expedition.

Chapter 11
A Matter of Honesty

On March 23, 1806, the Corps of Discovery left Fort Clatsop and began the return trip to St. Louis. Many Indians continued to crowd the riverbank to watch as the explorers passed by their villages. Lewis wrote that while most of them seemed friendly, some of them appeared sullen and "illy disposed." He added that "one of them had the insolence to cast stones down the bank at two of the men who happened to be a little detached from the party at that time."

One day early in April, Private John Shields remained behind the expedition to purchase a dog from a group of Indians. Later, as he hurried to catch up with the others, two warriors stopped him and attempted to take the dog. Shields had only a knife with which to protect himself. Nevertheless, he was determined not to be robbed. When the Indians realized the explorer was prepared to fight back, they left the dog and fled into the woods.

That same day, Lewis had a similar problem. An Indian informed him that some warriors from a nearby village had stolen his dog, Scannon. Angrily, the captain sent three well-armed men in pursuit. He ordered them to fire on the thieves if "they made the least resistance or difficulty in surrendering the dog." After a two-mile chase, Lewis' men overtook the Indians who, fearing capture and punishment, released Scannon and fled.

Lewis and Clark were upset and concerned by this outbreak of stealing. They ordered their guards to keep all Indians away from their camp. Lewis commented angrily that "if they made any further attempts to steal our property, or insulted our men, we should put them to instant death."

The chief of the village that stole Scannon was ashamed of what his men had done. He apologized for their behavior and said these "two very bad men" were not representative of his people. He hoped the white men would not blame his entire village for this crime. Lewis said the chief "appeared to be a man of consideration, and we had reason to believe much

Scannon was Lewis' black Newfoundland dog.

respected by the neighboring tribes." The captains decided to accept the apology and presented the chief with a small peace medal. They hoped their relationship with the Indians would now resume its usual friendly nature.

Travel up the Columbia was much more difficult than rowing with the current had been. Water from the spring thaw had swollen the river and increased the force of the rapids. The men traveled only seven miles in three days during the month of April.

The explorers portaged around the worst places in the river. They used ropes to lift their canoes to the tops of thundering waterfalls. On April 12, one canoe was lost as the men struggled to hoist it from the river below. They watched helplessly as it plummeted down the cascade to be destroyed in the white water below.

To avoid more losses on the river, the captains decided to purchase horses and carry their baggage overland. However, dealing with the tribes in the Narrows and the Cascades was very difficult. The expedition was short of trade goods and the Indians demanded high prices for even the poorest animals. Finally, after a great deal of bargaining, the captains were able to purchase ten horses to transport their supplies.

Problems with thieves continued to plague the expedition. After several things had already been taken, Lewis caught an Indian attempting to steal the "iron socket of a canoe pole." The captain was furious and wrote:

> I . . . gave him several severe blows, and made the men kick him out of camp. I now informed the Indians that I would shoot the first of them that attempted to steal an article from us; that we were not afraid to fight them; that I had it in my power at that moment to kill them all and set fire to their houses; but it was not my wish to treat them with severity provided they would let my property alone.

Though angry and frustrated, Lewis did not want to treat

the Indians unjustly. He wanted only the guilty ones punished. The village chiefs shared his concern and were very upset by the behavior of some of their people. When told about the thefts, the leaders "hung their heads and said nothing."

On April 20, Lewis and Clark met an Indian who offered to guide them back to the land of the Nez Perce. He assured the captains that the tribes further ahead on the river would deal with the expedition in a more honorable manner. This was welcome news. The explorers were eager to return to country where they did not have to be constantly on guard against thieves.

Lewis and Clark arrived at the mouth of the Walla Walla River on April 27. They visited the village of Yellept, an important chief of the Wallawallas. The explorers had visited these Indians before in October of 1805. Yellept was delighted to see the white men again. He insisted they stay with his people and rest a few days. The captains were eager to be on their way, but agreed to remain overnight.

The men of the expedition wanted to trade with the Indians for food. Since the white men's supply of trade goods was low, the captains exchanged medical treatment for the things they needed. Captain Clark saw patients with a variety of ailments. Among them was a man with a broken arm and another with rheumatism in his knee. The most common problem was an irritation of the eyes. Lewis wrote that this was the "universal complaint with all the natives we have seen west of the Rocky Mountains." The captains thought the ailment may have been caused by fine sand or the glare of the sun on the water where the Indians fished. Clark gave his patients some "eye-water" which seemed to relieve their discomfort. Lewis wrote, "My friend, Captain Clark, is their favorite physician . . . " The Indians were very grateful for the medical attention they received.

The Yakimas performed tribal dances to entertain members of the expedition.

At times like these, the captains often wished they had more medical training. To avoid harming anyone with improper treatment, Lewis and Clark said they always took "care to give them no article which can possibly injure them."

Chief Yellept invited some Yakima Indians to join his people and meet the members of the expedition. About 100 Yakima men and a few women arrived shortly before sunset. The Indians formed a half-circle around the camp of Lewis and Clark. They enjoyed watching as the white men danced to the music of Cruzat's fiddle. Later, the Indians took their turn and entertained by performing dances of their own. The celebration continued far into the night.

On May 1, three young warriors from the Wallawalla village returned a steel trap they had found to Lewis and Clark. The captains, who had recently encountered so much stealing, were overwhelmed by the honesty of these people. They were further amazed on several other occasions when small articles they had lost were returned to them. Lewis described the Wallawallas as "the most hospitable, honest, and sincere people that we have met with in our voyage."

Chapter 12

Back to the Bitterroots

The Corps of Discovery had only traveled a short distance from the Wallawalla village when they met some of their old Nez Perce friends. One of these the captains had nicknamed "Chief Bighorn" because he wore the horn of a bighorn sheep hanging from his left arm. Bighorn had learned of the return of the white men and set out with ten of his warriors to meet them.

After a brief visit, the expedition continued until they arrived at the camp of another Nez Perce chief. This man was known as "Cut Nose" because of a wound he received in a battle with some Shoshoni Indians. While in the village, Clark again provided medical treatment for people suffering from irritated eyes.

The expedition was now only a short distance from the camp of Chief Twisted Hair. That was where they had left their horses and saddles the previous year. The captains were eager to reclaim their property and begin the recrossing of the Bitterroot Range.

Chief Cut Nose accompanied Lewis and Clark to the camp of Twisted Hair. The captains expected a warm welcome from the old chief. However, they were greeted in a very cold, unfriendly manner. Twisted Hair seemed angry and shouted at his guests. Being unfamiliar with the language, Lewis and Clark were very confused and alarmed by this strange behavior. They soon learned that the rage of the old chief was not directed at them. The cause of the outburst was the presence of Chief Cut Nose. The two Nez Perce leaders had recently been involved in a violent argument over the expedition's horses. Cut Nose and several other chiefs were upset because the white men had entrusted their belongings to Twisted Hair. The quarreling had continued until the old chief could stand it no longer. He agreed to divide the care of the horses among the other leaders. As a result, the animals were scattered about and now had to be recollected. Twisted Hair invited the captains to remain in his village until this could be accomplished.

The chief explained that the cache which contained the expedition's saddles had been flooded by the river that spring. He said that some of the contents may have been washed away before the mishap was discovered by his people. When the open cache was found, the chief had ordered his men to move the saddles to a new storage place on higher ground where they remained safely hidden.

On the evening of May 9, the Nez Perce warriors returned to camp with the expedition's horses and saddles. Most of the animals were in excellent condition. However, only about half of the saddles had been recovered after the flood. The captains were certain the Nez Perce had done their best to safeguard the things placed in their care. They were grateful to Twisted Hair's people for their help.

Indians visited the expedition's campsite at the end of each day's travel. Sometimes they brought gifts of food or provided shelter for the explorers. On May 10, Lewis and Clark met a Nez Perce chief who gave them some salmon and dried roots. He also made a large tepee available for their use while in his village.

Chief Twisted Hair

As they enjoyed the hospitality of the Nez Perce camp, the captains were visited by several other important tribal leaders. The gathering became so large, Lewis and Clark decided to hold a council and explain the reasons for their expedition. They also wanted to tell the Indians about the United States, its government, and its plans for the future of the Oregon Country. The captains emphasized President Jefferson's desire for peace among all the tribes. They promised trading posts would be established where the Nez Perce could obtain many wonderful things. Clark wrote that the Indians seemed "highly pleased" with this information.

One young boy was so impressed he brought a fine mare and her colt as gifts for the captains. He said the animals should be regarded as proof of his intentions to follow the white men's advice. Their message had brought great joy to his people.

The Indians told Lewis and Clark that it was too early in the year for them to attempt a crossing of the Bitterroot Range. The passes were still filled with snow and there was no grass to provide food for the horses. It was suggested the expedition remain encamped until the next full moon. That would mean a delay of almost a month in their progress.

Remembering the ordeal they encountered the last time they crossed these mountains, the captains decided to follow the Indians' advice. They chose a campsite near the Clearwater River where hunting was good and salmon would soon arrive from the Pacific Ocean. They remained there from May 14 to June 10.

On May 22, Clark wrote that Sacajawea's baby, Pomp, had become "dangerously ill." The child had survived all the hardships of the expedition but now he had developed a high fever, severe diarrhea, and a swelling in his neck and throat. The captains gave him medicine and applied a poultice of hot onions to his neck. They changed the poultice at regular in-

Pomp

tervals throughout the day and night. Despite their efforts, the baby's condition continued to become worse during the next week. Lewis and Clark were both worried about Pomp and wrote about his illness each day in their journals. Finally, on May 27, the child seemed much better though his neck was still swollen and Clark feared a growing abscess behind his ear. The captain treated the swelling with a mixture of the resin of long-leafed pine, bees' wax, and bear's oil. By June 8, the medicine had done its work and Pomp was pronounced "nearly well."

With the youngest member of their expedition out of danger, the attention of Lewis and Clark could again be directed to preparations for their recrossing of the Bitterroot Range. They wanted to collect as much food as possible before beginning the trip. The captains sent hunters out each day. Sacajawea gathered and dried fennel roots. Clark said the roots were about as big as a man's finger and could be eaten fresh, roasted, or boiled.

Trading with the Indians was now extremely difficult. The explorers were so short of trade goods the captains tore the buttons from their coats to exchange for some roots and bread.

While visiting the Nez Perce village, Drewyer discovered a tomahawk that had been stolen from the expedition. This tomahawk was important because it had belonged to the late Sergeant Floyd. Captain Clark had saved it as a memento for the sergeant's friends. The Nez Perce had acquired the tomahawk by trading with the thief who had taken it. Drewyer was unable to recover the weapon because the present owner had just died and his relatives intended to bury it with him. Clark refused to give up and finally persuaded the Indians to trade the stolen article for a handkerchief and two strands of beads. The village chiefs also helped in this matter by providing the family of the dead man with two horses to be killed at the gravesite according to tribal custom.

Though still short of supplies, the members of the expedition were in high spirits and ready to move on by June 10. The men loaded their baggage onto the horses and traveled toward the prairie where they had first met the Nez Perce.

On June 16, the Corps of Discovery arrived at Hungry Horse Creek. The captains decided to camp there and allow their horses to graze. They were afraid it would be many days before they came to another place with enough grass to feed their animals.

Even though the men of the expedition had delayed their journey until later in the spring, they still encountered a great deal of snow in the mountains. The snow had become firm enough to support the weight of their horses. However, it covered the trail and made it difficult to know in which direction to travel.

Lewis and Clark had only traveled about three miles from Hungry Horse Creek when they encountered snow that was from 12 to 15 feet deep. The captains realized there was no hope of finding grass for their horses in the near future. The animals could not go more than five days without food. They were too important to the success of the expedition to take chances with their welfare. Without horses, the valuable records and scientific collections could not be transported across the mountains.

The trail had become almost impossible to follow in the deep snow. Familiar landmarks were buried and the men were afraid of becoming lost.

The captains considered the matter carefully and decided to return to Hungry Horse Creek. Lewis wrote that "this is the first time since we have been on this long tour that we have ever been compelled to retreat or make a retrograde march."

Before returning, the men stored their baggage beside the

trail so the horses would not have to carry it back and forth. They built scaffolds to hold the carefully wrapped bundles above the snow. They were dissappointed by the further delay but realized that carelessness at this point could cost them everything.

After returning to the grassland, the captains sent Drewyer and another man back to the Nez Perce village for help. Lewis and Clark realized they would have to wait a very long time for all the snow to melt. They wanted to be on their way again as soon as possible and hoped the Indians would be able to guide them safely across the snow-covered mountains. They told Drewyer to offer guns and horses in return for the services of Indian guides.

The first few days back at Hungry Horse Creek presented more problems. One of the men cut his leg very badly with a large knife. Lewis had difficulty stopping the bleeding. Another accident occurred when a horse lost its footing and fell with its rider down the steep bank of the creek. Though considerably shaken up, neither horse nor rider were injured in this mishap.

On June 23, Drewyer returned with three Nez Perce guides. One of them was the brother of Chief Cut Nose. Clark wrote that all three young men were "of good character and much respected by their nation."

The expedition returned to the place where the baggage had been stored beside the trail. The men found everything exactly as they had left it. Though the level of the snow had gone down about seven feet, the trail was still impossible to follow without the help of the Nez Perce.

The guides said they should travel quickly because food for the horses was still some distance away. They wanted to reach the grass before making camp that evening.

Clark wrote that the guides led the expedition "along the steep sides of tremendous mountains entirely covered with

The Corps of Discovery recrossed the rugged Bitterroot Range.

snow..." Finally, late in the evening, they reached the place where they could graze their horses.

By June 27, the Corps of Discovery was entirely surrounded by towering, snow-covered mountains. Clark wrote that without their guides, "it would have seemed impossible ever to have escaped" from the white wilderness that encompassed them.

The men were relieved when on June 29 they finally reached the end of the trail across the mountains. They arrived at a hot springs where the Indians had created a bathing area by "stopping the river with stone and mud." Everyone enjoyed relaxing in the springs. Captain Lewis could only remain in the hottest water about ten minutes. The heat caused him to sweat profusely. The Indians stayed in the hot springs as long as possible and then plunged into the icy water of a nearby creek. After doing this several times, they ended with a warm bath.

Chapter 13
Danger Along Marias River

After recrossing the Rocky Mountains, the captains decided to divide their expedition into two parts. This would enable them to explore a much greater area than they had on their previous visit. Lewis would take some men and travel north by the shortest route to the Great Falls of the Missouri. He would explore the area around Marias River and recover the equipment and supplies the Corps of Discovery had stored there on their trip to the ocean. Lewis would then travel eastward and meet Clark and the others at the juncture of the Missouri and Yellowstone rivers.

Captain Clark and the remaining members of the expedition were to travel south to reclaim the baggage and canoes stored near the Jefferson River. After making any necessary repairs on the canoes, ten of the men would use them to travel directly to the meeting with Captain Lewis. Clark and the rest of his men would continue overland to the place where the Yellowstone River closely approaches the Three Forks of the Missouri. There, they would build several canoes in which to complete their journey to the meeting at the juncture of the two rivers.

On July 3, Lewis departed with the Nez Perce guides and nine members of the expedition. The Indians were now becoming eager to return home. They said they had traveled too close to land occupied by their enemies, the Minnetarees. They were afraid of being attacked if they remained with the white men much longer. Lewis wrote that at noon on July 4, he "smoked a pipe with these friendly people and . . . bid them adiew." He added that, "These affectionate people, our guides, betrayed every emotion of unfeigned regret at separating from us." He gave the brother of Chief Cut Nose a small peace medal and a gun. This so pleased the young man, he presented the captain with his most precious possession. This was the gift of his own name. Lewis gratefully accepted the name which meant "White Bearskin Folded." The transfer of a name indicated great respect and admiration. This honor had been given once before on the expedition when Cameahwait presented his name to Captain Clark.

Lewis and his men noticed large herds of buffalo near the Great Falls of the Missouri. Their horses were unfamiliar with these huge animals and appeared afraid of them. On the morning of July 12, the men awoke to discover their horses had disappeared during the night. Lewis thought perhaps they had been frightened away by buffalo wandering too near the camp. He immediately sent some men to recover the lost animals. After searching most of the day, the explorers returned with ten of the seventeen missing horses. Drewyer and another man went out to find the remaining seven.

While awaiting the return of Drewyer, Lewis and his men continued their journey along the river. Soon they arrived at a place they had camped the year before. They had no trouble locating the cache where they had stored their supplies. Lewis discovered the river had flooded the cache and destroyed several of the articles inside. These included the captains animals skins and all the plant specimens he had collected. Fortunately, the maps of the Missouri and other papers remained unharmed.

On July 15, Drewyer returned without the horses he set out to find. He said that he had located an abandoned Indian campsite. He thought the camp, which contained 15 lodges, had been moved about the same time the expedition's horses had disappeared. Lewis began to suspect that Indians rather than buffalo were responsible for the loss of the animals. He thought that a hunting party may have discovered the camp of the white men and attempted to take their horses. However, since enough animals had been recaptured to transport their supplies, the captain decided to continue his exploration and leave the Indians alone.

Earlier that same day, Lewis had sent Private McNeal ahead to locate another cache and the pirogue that had been stored along the river. McNeal returned late in the evening with a broken gun and a report of his narrow escape from a grizzly bear. He explained that he had suddenly noticed the grizzly while riding past some thick brush. The bear had remained concealed until the explorer was only about ten feet away. McNeal's horse panicked and threw him directly in front of the grizzly. The fierce animal raised up on its hind legs and prepared to attack. Terrified, McNeal grabbed his gun and clubbed the bear over the head. The strength of the blow broke the gun and temporarily stunned the grizzly. This gave the explorer time to run and frantically climb a nearby tree. The bear soon recovered and followed McNeal to the tree where it waited angrily for him to climb down. Late in the evening, it seemed to lose interest and gave up the attack. As soon as it was gone, McNeal immediately returned to the safety of the camp.

McNeal's report and the presence of Indians in the area caused Lewis to begin to worry about the safety of his men.

Private McNeal was attacked by a grizzly bear.

On July 26, the captain divided his followers into two parties. Drewyer led one group along the bank of Marias River while Lewis and the other men explored the nearby hills. The captain had not gone far when he noticed several riders sitting motionless on a hilltop. They appeared to be studying something on the river below them. Using his spyglass, Lewis was able to identify the riders as a group of Blackfoot Indians. He counted at least 30 horses but could not be certain of the number of men. He began to suspect that the object of their interest was the group of explorers led by Drewyer.

The Indians were so involved in what they were doing, they failed to notice the approach of Lewis and his men. When they finally became aware of the white men, they appeared to become confused and alarmed.

Lewis was afraid the warriors were preparing for an attack. His first impulse was to run away. However, he realized that flight would immediately label the explorers as enemies and provoke the Indians to chase them. Furthermore, even if he and his men managed to escape, the angry warriors could still return and attack Drewyer and the others who were still unaware of the danger.

The captain decided to stand his ground and attempt a peaceful meeting. The explorers advanced until they were within a half mile of the Blackfeet. As they drew near, one of the warriors charged toward them on his horse at full speed. When he was within a hundred yards of Lewis and his men, the Indian halted and stared intently at them. He may have been sent to determine the number and strength of the potential new enemies. After a few seconds, the rider turned his horse and dashed back to his companions on the hilltop.

Lewis held out his hand and beckoned the Indians to join him for a meeting. Finally, all the warriors mounted their horses and rode toward the explorers. Lewis feared the Indians might outnumber his men and attempt to rob them. He felt much more confident when he was able to see there were only eight riders in the group.

The Blackfeet wanted to begin the council immediately by smoking the pipe of peace. Lewis found it difficult to trust these Indians because they seemed nervous and uncomfortable in the presence of the white men. He was afraid there might be more warriors in the area and wanted time to gather all the explorers together in case of trouble. He requested that the meeting be delayed until he could send for Drewyer and the rest of his men. The captain justified this by saying that Drewyer carried the white men's special pipe which was a necessary part of all their formal councils. The Blackfeet appeared to accept this excuse. One of them decided to accompany the man Lewis sent to bring back Drewyer.

It was becoming late in the day and Lewis suggested that everyone should camp together beside the river. The Indians agreed and invited the explorers to share a large tepee they had brought with them. As the camp was prepared, Drewyer's party arrived with the men sent to find them. With everyone now present, the council was soon ready to begin.

The Blackfeet explained they had traveled here with their people on a buffalo hunt. The others were camped along the river near the Rocky Mountains. They had seen another large group of Indian hunters moving in this direction. They should arrive in a day or so.

Lewis presented gifts of friendship to the Blackfoot leaders. Then he delivered his usual speech about the United States and its plans to establish trading posts in the area. He also expressed Jefferson's wish that all Indians live together in peace. He stressed that this included putting an end to the hostility between the tribes on this side of the mountains and those like the Nez Perce on the other side.

Lewis ordered the Blackfoot warrior to drop his gun.

The Blackfeet seemed to agree with what they were told. The council continued late into the night and ended with another smoking of the peace pipe.

Lewis was exhausted after this long day. He entered the tepee and almost immediately fell into a deep sleep. Shortly before daylight, he was suddenly awakened by a loud disturbance outside.

Rushing from the tepee, the captain saw Drewyer struggling with an Indian who was attempting to steal his gun. Lewis raced back for his own weapon just in time to see it also being taken. The captain drew his pistol and ordered the thief to halt and drop the gun. Though he did not know the language, the warrior understood the white man's meaning. Realizing he could not escape, he did as he was told.

By the time Lewis returned, Drewyer had already recovered his gun. However, the attacker had escaped with his entire supply of ammunition.

Two other members of the expedition were now returning to camp with their weapons after chasing and overpowering the Indians who had stolen them. They reported that they had killed one of the thieves in the struggle.

The Blackfeet, realizing they had failed in their attempt to steal the white men's guns, now decided to take their horses instead. They drove the animals from camp by shouting and waving their arms. Lewis ordered his men to shoot the Indians if necessary to regain the horses.

The explorers pursued the Blackfeet along the river bank. Lewis chased two of the thieves, one of which was the same man who had attempted to take his gun. Eventually, the captain became too out of breath to continue. He shouted a warning that he intended to shoot if the Indians did not stop immediately. One of the warriors jumped behind a rock for safety. Lewis shot the other one who fired back and then also managed to crawl behind the rock.

The captain had not taken time to arm himself properly for the chase. He had left his extra ammunition behind. Afraid to attack the Indians with only a single shot left in his pistol, Lewis was forced to return to camp. Once there, he burned all the bows and arrows the Blackfeet had not taken with them. Since the thieves had managed to escape with only two guns, the explorers were relatively safe from immediate attack.

Lewis was afraid the six remaining Blackfeet would eventually return with a war party to continue the battle. He decided to lead his men back to the Missouri as quickly as possible. He hoped that Captain Clark's men had by now recovered the canoes and were traveling on the river in his direction. With luck, Lewis and his men could intercept the canoes and use them for a quick escape from danger.

Lewis and his followers rode their horses "as hard as they would bear" toward the Missouri. They continued traveling far into the night stopping only for a short rest and a little food. On July 28, they arrived at the bluffs overlooking the river. They heard gunfire in the distance which they were certain came from army rifles. The men rode to the riverbank and were overjoyed to see canoes traveling toward them. They quickly released their horses and joined the ten explorers sent by Clark to take the canoes to the juncture of the Missouri and Yellowstone rivers.

Chapter 14
A Near-Fatal Mistake

Lewis and the others traveled to the entrance of Marias River where they had left one of their pirogues the previous year. They intended to repair any damage the boat may have suffered and take it along with them to their meeting with Captain Clark. However, the weather had so severely damaged the pirogue, it was impossible to salvage it. The men took the iron works and other things which might still be useful and abandoned the rest.

The explorers lost no time in traveling to the juncture of the Missouri and Yellowstone rivers. They wanted to rejoin the rest of the expedition as soon as possible. When they arrived on August 7, they were disappointed to discover they had just missed Captain Clark and the others. Lewis found a note attached to a pole in the abandoned campsite. Clark had written it to explain that mosquitoes and poor hunting had prevented his men from remaining in this area. They had moved their camp and were waiting a few miles further along the river.

Lewis ordered his men to resume their journey on the Missouri. He was certain they would soon locate Clark and the others. After traveling about eight miles with no sign of the expedition, Lewis decided it was time to allow a rest. His men were exhausted. They had been given no free time since leaving the Rocky Mountains. Their clothing was completely worn out and they needed time to tan fresh skins to replace the rags they were now wearing. The canoes had also been damaged and must be repaired. Though time was important, Lewis decided a short delay was necessary for the welfare of his men. He located a sandy beach where the canoes could be pulled from the water and gave the explorers a break from their long, difficult journey.

By August 11, the men were again ready to return to the river. As they traveled in their newly-repaired canoes, Captain Lewis noticed a large herd of elk. He decided to take Cruzat and go ashore to hunt.

On the riverbank, the two men separated to approach the elk from different directions. Lewis entered a thickly wooded area and was about to fire his rifle when he was shot in the left thigh slightly below the hip. The ball passed completely through his leg missing the bone and creating a painful wound. When he recovered from the first shock of the injury, the captain thought Cruzat, who had poor eyesight, had probably mistaken him for an elk. The brown, leather clothing he wore had caused him to resemble an animal hidden among the trees.

Fearing more gunfire, Lewis angrily shouted, " . . . you shot me!" His cry brought no response from the suddenly silent forest around him. After shouting several more times without receiving an answer, the captain's anger turned to fear. Perhaps the shot had not come from Cruzat's rifle. It may have been fired by hostile Indians who now enjoyed watching their victim panic as they prepared for a final attack. Lewis' eyes scanned the trees for any sign of movement. His ears strained to detect any sound to indicate the location of his hidden enemies. The forest remained quiet and peaceful in sharp contrast to the recent explosion of violence.

Captain Lewis was nearly killed in a hunting accident.

The captain wanted to return immediately to the safety of the canoes. But he still wondered what had happened to his companion. Perhaps Cruzat was still hunting and unaware of the danger in the area. Lewis ran toward the river as best he could with his injured leg. As he went, he shouted repeated warnings to the other hunter.

When he reached the canoes, Lewis immediately ordered his men to help him search for Cruzat. The captain's wound had become so painful it was now impossible for him to walk. He was forced to wait in a canoe while the others entered the forest without him. Still fearing another attack, the captain later wrote that he armed himself and prepared "to sell my life as dearly as possible."

After about 20 minutes, the explorers returned with Cruzat. They had found no Indians in the area. Cruzat was extremely upset and said that if he had shot the captain, it had certainly been by mistake. After leaving Lewis, he said he had killed an elk in the forest. He denied hearing shouts or anything else that might have indicated danger. Lewis did not completely accept this story. He wrote in his journal that "I do not believe that the fellow did it intentionally but after finding that he had shot me, he was anxious to conceal his knowledge of having done so." The captain dressed his wound as well as he could and traveled on with his men to rejoin Clark and the expedition.

Chapter 15
Smoke Signals Near the Yellowstone

On August 12, the entire Corps of Discovery was reunited. Captain Clark was concerned when he discovered his partner had been injured. Lewis recounted his adventures during their separation and assured Clark that he would be well again in "20 or 30 days."

Captain Clark also had experiences to share. When the two leaders had separated, he had taken 22 members of the expedition with him including Sacajawea, Pomp, and Lewis' dog, Scannon. Clark's first destination was the Jefferson River where he intended to recover the baggage stored there in 1805. The explorers followed a Flathead Indian trail that was much shorter and better than the old route of the expedition. However, when they reached a broad, level plain, the trail became confusing with tracks of Indians going in all directions. Fortunately, Sacajawea was able to help. She recognized the area as one she had visited during her childhood. She said her people often came there to dig camas and trap beaver. She led the explorers through a pass in the mountains now known as Gibbon's Pass and by July 8, they arrived at the Two Forks of the Jefferson River.

The men soon located the caches where they had stored their supplies. They were especially eager to recover the chewing tobacco which they had been without for several months. Clark wrote that they "... became so impatient to be chewing it that they scarcely gave themselves time to take their saddles off their horses before they were off to the deposit."

The explorers found their baggage exactly as they had left it. The canoes were also found in good condition except for one which had a large hole in the side and a split in the bow.

The canoe was soon repaired and the men ready to move on. Clark divided them into two groups. Sergeant Ordway took nine men and traveled in the canoes to the meeting with Captain Lewis. Clark took the rest of the men and traveled by horseback to explore the Yellowstone River and its meeting with the Missouri.

Clark's men had no trouble locating food as they traveled overland. There were large herds of elk, deer, and antelope. The captain also discovered there were numerous beaver and bighorn sheep in the area.

On July 14, the explorers crossed the Gallatin River. They had just left the area where Sacajawea had been captured by the Minnetarees. Clark now found trails leading toward two different mountain passes. Uncertain which path to follow, he again turned to Sacajawea. She recommended the southern route, now called Bozeman Pass, as the best entrance to the valley of the Yellowstone River. Taking the Indian woman's advice, the explorers crossed the mountains and soon arrived at their destination.

During most of this time, the horses had been walking on sharp stones and gravel. Their feet had become extremely sore and tender. On July 16, the captain encountered two grizzly bears which he decided to chase. However, he was forced to give up the pursuit after riding only about two miles into the rugged plain because his horse became too lame to continue.

Sacajawea led the explorers through Bozeman Pass.

Clark decided he must help the suffering animals if they were to remain useful to the expedition. He wrote that he "... had moccasins made of green buffalo skin and put on their feet, which seems to relieve them very much in passing over the stony plains."

Clark's men had only glimpsed one Indian since the departure of their Nez Perce guides. Then, on July 18, the captain observed smoke rising from the plains near the Rocky Mountains. Unable to interpret the signals, he thought perhaps the Crow Indians had discovered the presence of the white men and were sending an invitation to trade. He hoped the Crows had not mistaken his men for enemies and were spreading the alarm among the neighboring tribes.

The next day, Charbonneau saw an Indian across the river but was unable to discover his reason for being there. The smoke signals continued causing Clark to become both curious and slightly uneasy.

The captain now decided to travel on the Yellowstone River instead of continuing by horseback. He ordered several of his men to locate trees suitable for making large canoes. However, a careful search of the area produced no trees of the necessary size. Clark decided to make two small canoes instead and lash them together to form a larger vessel.

On the morning of July 21, as the explorers prepared to work on their canoes, Clark was informed that 24 of their horses were missing. The captain, fearing they had been stolen by Indians, immediately sent Charbonneau and two others to recover them. The men returned a few hours later and reported they had found no sign of the animals.

Two days later, Sergeant Pryor found an Indian moccasin and a small piece of a robe near their campsite. Another explorer reported that he had discovered the tracks of horses headed in the direction of the open plains. The animals seemed to be moving very rapidly. This information convinced Captain Clark that the horses had been taken by Indians. He realized that there was no longer any hope of recovering them. He was thankful that the Indians had managed to steal only half their horses and not all of them.

The captain ordered Sergeant Pryor and two other men to take the remaining horses overland to the Mandan Indian villages. He also asked Pryor to keep a journal to record "... courses, distances, water courses, soil productions, and animals" encountered on this journey.

By July 24, the canoes were finished and loaded with the expedition's baggage and supplies. The explorers had not traveled far on the river when they encountered rapids. The canoes began to fill with water and the men were forced to go ashore to dry their possessions.

On the beach, they were met by Sergeant Pryor who had

returned because he was having a difficult time with the horses. The animals had originally belonged to Indians who had trained them to hunt buffalo. The horses had learned their lessons well. Each time the explorers approached a herd of buffalo, the horses attempted to pursue and surround them. They persisted in this behavior despite all efforts to stop them.

After careful consideration of the problem, Clark decided there was only one possible solution. He assigned another explorer to accompany Sergeant Pryor. The new man would ride ahead of the others and chase the buffalo away before the horses became aware of them. Satisfied with this plan, Pryor once again departed and continued his journey to the Mandan villages.

On July 25, Clark and his men arrived at a remarkable sandstone formation on the south side of the river. The tower-like structure was nearly 200 feet tall. The captain decided to name the landmark Pompey's Pillar after the young child of Sacajawea and Charbonneau. Clark climbed to the top of the formation where he was rewarded with a magnificent view of "two low mountains and the Rocky Mountains covered with snow." The captain discovered that "The Indians have made two piles of stone on the top of this tower. The natives have engraved on the face of this rock the figures of animals . . . " Clark decided to add his own mark to those already decorating Pompey's Pillar. He carefully engraved his name and the date, July 25, 1806.

By the first of August, the explorers had reached the juncture of the Yellowstone and Missouri rivers. This was the place where Clark had agreed to meet Lewis and the rest of the expedition. Since Clark had arrived early, he ordered his men to camp beside the river and use the time to replenish their food supply. However, it soon became apparent that both camping and hunting were impossible in this place. The

Bighorn Sheep

area was filled with mosquitoes whose relentless attacks continued day and night. When the captain attempted to shoot a bighorn sheep, the insects bothered him so much he was unable to properly aim his rifle. Scannon, who spent most of his time in a tent, howled in pain from the bites and poor little Pomp's face was red and swollen. The captain decided the camp had to be moved to a new place along the river. Leaving a note for Lewis attached to a pole, Clark ordered his men to load the canoes and leave the area immediately.

On August 8, the captain noticed two buffalo skin canoes traveling behind him on the river. When the boats were close enough, Clark was astonished to recognize Sergeant Pryor and his men. He immediately wondered what had happened to the horses they had been taking to the Mandan villages.

Pryor soon explained that on the second night after his departure, he and his men had camped beside a large creek. They had allowed the horses to graze freely on the lush grass beside the water. In the morning, all the animals had disappeared. The explorers had discovered tracks within 100 paces of their camp where Indians had caught and driven off the horses. After following the thieves for about ten miles, Pryor realized that his men could never overtake the Indians on foot. He ordered the explorers to return to camp and carry their baggage back to the Yellowstone River. They eventually arrived near Pompey's Pillar where they constructed two canoes from the hide of a buffalo they had killed.

On the way to rejoin Captain Clark, a wolf had bitten Pryor's hand as he slept in camp beside the river. The vicious animal had also attempted to bite another man before it was finally killed. Clark noticed that Pryor's hand was healing properly and appeared nearly recovered.

The captain named a small river south of Pompey's Pillar Pryor's River in honor of the sergeant who had tried so hard to carry out his orders.

Chapter 16
Home Again

After all the members of the expedition were reunited on August 12, the explorers abandoned the buffalo skin canoes and everyone traveled together in the dugouts. When they stopped to rest for the night, Lewis was too stiff and sore from his recent injury to go ashore. He slept uncomfortably in the boat he had ridden in all day.

On August 24, the Corps of Discovery passed by the "Minnatarees' grand village." Many Indians turned out to watch the return of the white explorers. Traveling on, Lewis and Clark soon arrived at the Mandan villages where they intended to camp.

When they reached shore, the captains sent Charbonneau to invite the Mandan and Minnetaree chiefs to a council. Drewyer was sent to the lower Mandan village to invite Rene Jussome, a Frenchman Lewis and Clark had met in 1804. Jussome would be able to serve as an interpreter during the meeting.

Many Indians attended the council held by the white explorers. Clark wrote that after smoking the customary pipe of peace, "I informed them that I still spoke the same words which we had spoken to them when we first arrived in their country."

The captains asked some of the chiefs to return with them and learn about the United States first hand. They invited these Indians to:

> ... visit their Great Father, the President of the U. States, and to hear his own counsels and receive his gifts ... also to see the population of a government which can, at their pleasure, protect and secure you from all your enemies ... and chastise all those who will shut their ears to his counsels.

Though the invitation was attractive, all of the chiefs refused to accept. They were afraid of encountering their enemies, the Sioux, if they traveled on the river with the expedition.

The captains persisted in their efforts to persuade at least one of the chiefs to return with them. They asked Rene Jussome to use his influence to help. The Frenchman managed to convince Chief Sheheke, also known as Big White, to accompany Lewis and Clark. The chief agreed to go if he could take his wife and son along with him. The captains were happy to have Sheheke and his family as their guests for the journey home.

Charbonneau decided that he and his family would remain with the Mandans when Lewis and Clark left the village. He was no longer needed as an interpreter and he did not know how to make a living in the United States. He was more comfortable with his life among the Indians. In 1807, Captain Lewis described Charbonneau as "A man of no peculiar merit. Was useful as an interpreter only, in which capacity he discharged his duties in good faith ... " Charbonneau was paid wages amounting to $500.33. He used the money to purchase a tent and a horse. Unlike her husband, Sacajawea received no pay for her contribution to the expedition.

Clark had grown very fond of little Pomp who he described as a "beautiful, promising child." The captain offered to take

Sacajawea and Pomp remained with Charbonneau in the Mandan village.

him to be raised and educated in St. Louis. The boy's parents refused at that time because they thought he was too young to be separated from his mother. They did agree to bring Pomp to St. Louis at a later date when he was old enough to stay with Clark who they realized could best provide a secure future for him.

On August 17, the Lewis and Clark Expedition left the Mandan villages for the last time. They were now accompanied by Chief Sheheke and his family. Rene Jussome also joined the travelers to take his family to St. Louis.

Chief Sheheke's people lined the shore to wave good-by to their leader. They would eagerly await his return to "repeat whatever their Great Father should say." The explorers fired a final salute from their rifles and set out on the Missouri toward home.

Traveling downstream was much easier and faster than struggling upstream against the current had been. The canoes were now able to cover from 70 to 80 miles a day.

On August 30, Captain Clark saw several Indians on horseback watching the expedition from a hill overlooking the river. Later, when the explorers went ashore to hunt, 80 or 90 armed warriors came out of the forest about a quarter of a mile downstream on the other side of the river. The Indians gave a salute of rifle fire which was immediately returned by the expedition. Clark feared the warriors were hostile Teton Sioux. He wanted to get close enough to identify them with as little danger to his men as possible.

Captain Clark took three interpreters and paddled a canoe to a sand bar that extended near the opposite shore. As soon as he arrived, he was joined by three young Indians. They introduced themselves as members of a band of Teton Sioux led by Black Buffalo. Clark recognized the name of the chief who had attempted to sieze the expedition's supplies in the fall of 1804. To avoid a second confrontation with these people, the captain knew he must immediately get and keep the upper hand. Any sign of fear or weakness could result in a swift attack.

In his sternest, most authoratative voice, Clark told the Indians he considered them to be "bad people" who had mistreated the expedition during their last visit. He added that the Tetons "had abused all whites who visited them since." He ordered them to stay on their own side of the river because "if any of them came near our camp we should kill them certainly."

The Indians noticed some corn in the explorers' canoe and asked if they could have some of it. Clark refused and said he was "determined to have nothing to do with these people."

Several more warriors gathered on the sand bar. Clark bravely held his ground and continued to show utter contempt for the Tetons. He said they:

> ... treated all white people who had visited them very badly—robbed them of their goods, and had wounded one man ... no more traders would be suffered to come to them and whenever white people wished to visit the nations above, they would come sufficiently strong to whip any villainous party who dared to oppose them.

Clark said that he was also aware of the Teton's plan to attack the Mandans. He warned that the Mandans and the Minnetarees were now well equipped with guns and were very able to defend themselves. Clark ordered the warriors to return to their chiefs and tell them "to keep away from the river or we should kill every one of them."

The captain's strategy proved successful. The Tetons were abashed at the outspokenness of the white man. Unwilling to test the strength of this opposition, they withdrew and began to ride away from the river. Several angry warriors shouted threats and challenges from the top of a small hill.

They were ignored by the explorers who breathed a sigh of relief and quickly continued on their way.

On September 4, the expedition revisited the gravesite of Sergeant Floyd. The men were upset to discover the grave had been opened and was now only about half filled with earth. They thought someone may have been looking for valuables buried with the body of their friend. The explorers carefully refilled the grave and once again said good-by to the only lost member of the Corps of Discovery.

The Teton Sioux confronted the expedition a second time.

Lewis and Clark met several traders and other travelers heading north from St. Lewis. These men told the captains that almost everyone in the United States had given them up as lost and almost forgotten about them. Most Americans would not be surprised to learn the entire expedition was buried on the hill with Sergeant Floyd. Only President Jefferson still had hopes for the survival of the Corps of Discovery. This disturbing news made the explorers even more eager to return home and prove the success of their mission.

Excitement increased as the expedition drew closer and closer to St. Louis. The men asked and received permission to fire a salute from their guns at each town they passed along the river. On September 20, the travelers arrived at the little French village of Charrette. Clark wrote that:

> Every person, both French and American, seemed to express great pleasure at our return, and acknowledged themselves much astonished in seeing us return. They informed us that we were supposed to have been lost long since . . .

On September 23, the triumphant Corps of Discovery arrived at St. Louis. Clark wrote "We suffered the party to fire off all their pieces as a salute to the town. We were met by all the village and received a hearty welcome from its inhabitants . . ." Lewis and Clark were home! They had made it possible for Jefferson's dream to become reality!

The expedition had taken two years and four months. The men had traveled well over 7,000 miles since they first left St. Louis. Most of that distance had been through unexplored wilderness. In accomplishing their mission, they had disproved the idea of a northwest passage across North America. However, they did establish a route to the Pacific Ocean. They had explored and recorded a wealth of information about the Louisiana Territory and the Oregon Country. There was now a path to lead American settlers west. The future states of Kansas, Missouri, Nebraska, Iowa, North Dakota, South Dakota, Montana, Idaho, Washington, and Oregon were about to be born. Thousands would follow in the footsteps of Lewis and Clark and owe a debt of thanks to these brave men who were the first.

Epilogue

As a result of their successful expedition, Lewis and Clark became the new heroes of the American West. Within hours of their arrival in St. Louis, eastern newspapers reported their triumphant return from the wilderness. Dinners, parties, parades, and speeches were given in their honor.

Congress rewarded the members of the Corps of Discovery with double pay for time spent on the frontier. The men were also given land. Lewis and Clark both received 1,600 acres and each of the others received 320 acres.

Clark rewarded Ben York, his friend and servant, with his freedom. There are two different accounts of the remainder of York's life. One says he worked successfully in a freight-hauling business in Tennessee. The other says he returned west to live with the Indians. Historians have yet to discover which of these stories is true.

After the excitement of their homecoming, the captains left St. Louis and went home to their families and friends. However, both men soon returned to the city to accept important governmental appointments.

The Territory of Louisiana was created in March, 1804 with St. Louis as its territorial capital. On March 3, 1807, Lewis was named Governor of the Louisiana Territory. One week later, Clark was made Brigadier General of the territorial militia and Superintendent of Indian Affairs.

Clark arrived in St. Louis in May, 1807. Almost immediately he arranged a meeting with the Osage and Sioux tribes to begin treaty negotiations. By September, he had also organized the militia to provide more effective protection for the newly established territory.

Several months later, Clark traveled to Virginia and married Julia Hancock whom he had courted before the expedition to the Pacific.

On March 8, 1808, while Clark was away on his honeymoon, Lewis rented a house in St. Louis which he intended to share with the newlyweds. However, the residence proved too small when the couple returned and the governor soon moved to other quarters. Though claiming to have fallen in love several times, Lewis remained unmarried throughout his life.

Clark had written a letter to Charbonneau on August 20, 1806 offering to raise and educate Jean Baptiste as his own child in St. Louis. He wrote, "As to your little son (my boy Pomp), you well know my fondness for him and my anxiety to take and raise him as my own child . . . " The letter also contained an offer to assist Charbonneau with land or trade goods in appreciation for his service to the expedition. It ended with the suggestion that if Charbonneau wished to comply, he should bring Sacajawea (referred to as "Janey") along to care for Pomp until he could safely be delivered to Clark.

The offer was accepted in 1808 when Charbonneau and Sacajawea arrived in St. Louis with their son. Clark kept his promise and provided an education for Jean Baptiste who eventually traveled to Europe to continue his studies. The interpreter's son became a man of culture and distinction. He returned home and for a time led the life of a mountain man in the American wilderness. He also became mayor of a town and operated a hotel in California.

Unfortunately, after the expedition, detailed records were not kept on the lives of many of the explorers. Sacajawea was one such person. Many historians believe that in 1811 she and her husband journeyed up the Missouri by boat with Manuel Lisa of the Missouri Fur Company. Another passenger on the boat, Henry Brackenridge, wrote the following entry in his journal:

> We have on board a Frenchman named Charbonet [sic], with him his wife, an Indian woman of the Snake nation, both of whom accompanied Lewis and Clark to the Pacific, and were of great service. The woman . . . had become sickly and longed to revisit her native country . . .

In 1812, John Luttig, clerk of the Missouri Fur Company, wrote about the death of "the wife of Charbonneau." He said she " . . . died of a putrid fever she was a good and the best woman in the fort . . . "

Clark reaffirmed the death of Sacajawea in 1825 when he compiled a list of the explorers indicating those who remained alive. Beside the Indian woman's name, he wrote the word "dead."

Lewis and Clark faced many problems as they worked to govern and protect the Louisiana Territory. The French who lived in the area argued with the American newcomers over land titles and mining claims. White settlers ignored Indian treaties and moved onto tribal land. Independent fur traders rebelled against the federal regulation of Indian trade. Governor Lewis created enemies as he tried to settle land claims and maintain fair trade policies with the Indians.

Clark, likewise, worked to deal fairly with the Indians. In June, 1808, he began construction of Fort Osage at the mouth of the Osage River. This fort would guard the Missouri River and keep unlicensed traders away from Indian villages. Late in 1808, Clark completed negotiations with the Osage and signed a treaty with the tribe.

Though Lewis and Clark worked together for common governmental objectives, public reaction differed toward the two men. Lewis was viewed as abrasive because of his introverted, sometimes moody personality. Clark, on the other hand, managed to avoid harsh criticism during this time.

Lewis' unpopularity reached its peak late in 1808 and early 1809. At that time, the British were attempting to incite an Indian war on the frontier near St. Louis. After a few small raids and the murder of several white men, settlers began traveling to St. Louis for protection. Lewis ordered troops into the threatened area placing a heavy call on Clark's newly established militia. By fast action, the governor managed to prevent further conflict and the settlers were soon able to return home. Lewis' success failed to turn the tide of public opinion against him. When war failed to erupt, militiamen complained that they had been called away from their homes and families unnecessarily. They added their voices to the opposition that already existed against the governor.

In addition to harsh criticism, Lewis was also plagued with financial problems. Soon after accepting his governmental post in St. Louis, he had purchased 5,700 acres of land near the town. He had used most of his money to place a $3,000 downpayment on the land which cost about a dollar an acre. Lewis called upon the federal government to cover the expenses of carrying out his official duties in the territory. He began to forward bills to Washington for payment. In the summer of 1809, a War Department clerk returned a bill for $18.70 to Lewis with a note saying it was "... drawn without authority" and "can not be paid at this Department." By the end of the summer, bills totaling $4,000 had been returned to the governor for payment. Lewis was forced to appease his creditors by giving them title to the land holdings he possessed.

Lewis was extremely upset and decided to travel to Washington and attempt to clear his reputation by explaining his expenditures in person. He decided that this was also the only hope he had of recovering the money lost in his payment of the contested bills.

Lewis departed for Washington on September 15, 1809. On October 10, he reached Grinder's Stand on the Natchez Trace in Tennessee. There, the man who had survived all the dangers and hardships of a long trip through an unexplored wilderness, met a mysterious death that still remains unexplained. There is equal evidence to support both suicide and murder. Clark tended to support the idea of suicide when he first heard of his friend's death. However, in later life, he changed his opinion and denied the possibility that Lewis took his own life.

After Lewis' death, Clark lost some of his enthusiasm for territorial government. He remained as brigidier general of the militia and accepted the job of inspector general. He did not seek reappointment as governor. Instead, he supported Benjamin Howard, a congressman from Kentucky, in his quest for that office. Howard received the appointment on April 7, 1809.

In 1809, Clark formed the St. Louis Missouri Fur Company with Manuel Lisa and several others. However, the new trading company was unable to survive the fierce competition of John Jacob Astor's already established traders. After several instances of poor judgment by the partners, the unsuccessful venture was dissolved in 1812.

On June 16, 1813, President James Madison appointed Clark governor of the Missouri Territory. Clark held this position until 1820 when Missouri became a state.

During his territorial governorship, Clark continued his attempts to keep peace among the Indians. He also worked to defend the area from foreign intervention. He used his own money to finance the construction of four gunboats to protect America's use of western waterways.

Clark's popularity began to decline when he stated his desire to assimilate the Indians into the American economy. Many settlers wanted to eliminate the tribes altogether and free their lands for new homesteads. The idea of forcing Native Americans to leave their ancestral homes was completely foreign to Clark who had spent most of his life attempting to understand and help the Indians.

Clark also received criticism when he revived Lewis' plan for granting exclusive trading privileges to a single American company. He thought such regulation was the only way to guarantee fair dealings with Indian tribes. However, St. Louis society viewed this policy as an unfair privilege that favored a few wealthy trading families. The criticism directed at Clark caused him to lose the race for governor when the state of Missouri was created in 1820.

Even though he had problems, Clark's life as a public figure was not over. In 1821, President James Monroe appointed him Superintendent of Indian Affairs. He held this post for the rest of his life. Clark continued to call upon the government to provide the Indians with land, education, and the opportunity to become productive American citizens.

On June 27, 1820, Julia Clark died after a two-year illness. On November 28, 1821, William married Julia's widowed second cousin, Mrs. Harriet Kennerly Radford. During his two marriages, Clark became the father of seven children. Five were born of his first marriage and two of his second. Harriet died in 1831 and three of the children also preceded their father in death.

Clark remained active almost to the end of his life. In his later years he was described as a "tall, robust old man with beetle- brows." The second leader of the Corps of Discovery died on September 1, 1838 at the home of his oldest son, Meriwether Lewis Clark. This was the child he had named in memory of his great friend who had accompanied him on the adventure of a lifetime. After Clark's death, a Missouri newspaper article dated September 3, 1838 commented, "... to such men falling around us will wring a sigh from every breast, and a tear from every eye."

The members of the Corps of Discovery are gone but their remarkable accomplishments will keep them alive forever in the pages of American history.

Acknowledgements

Myrtle A. Fisher

Ed and Sharon Holmblad

Orville Reddington

Merle Wells, Ph.D.

Charlene Wicks

Nancy Williamson

Index

Appalacian Mountains, 2
Astor, John Jacob, 133
Arikara Indians, 16
Beaverhead Rock, 46
Bighorn, Chief, 89
Big White. See Chief Sheheke
Birdwoman's River, 23
Bitterroot Range, 59–60, 89, 92, 94
Bitterroot River, 59
Black Buffalo, Chief, 124
Blackfoot Indians, 103–106
Bozeman Pass, 114
Brackenridge, Henry, 131
Cache, preparation of, 33–34
Cameahwait, Chief, 23, 51, 53–57, 100
Canada, 4
Cascade Mountains, 69
Celilo Falls, 67
Charbonneau, Jean Baptiste. See Pomp
Charbonneau, Toussaint, 20–21, 23–25, 30–31, 35–36, 39, 46, 55, 75, 115–116, 121–122, 130–131
Charbonneau, Toussaint Jr., 20
Charrette, 127
Chief Red Hair, 26

Chinook Indians, 70
Clark, General George Rogers, 5–6
Clark, Julia. See Julia Hancock
Clark, Meriwether Lewis, 135
Clark, William: preparation for journey, 5–7; with Charles Floyd, 10; on the Missouri River, 11; and the Teton Sioux, 11, 13–15; suffers from rheumatism, 16, 18; and the Arikara Indians, 16; at Fort Mandan, 17–18, 21, 23; given nickname, 26; at Yellowstone River, 27–28, 30–31; nearing Rocky Mountains, 31–32; at Marias River, 33; at Great Falls, 34, 39–40; at Three Forks, 43; on Jefferson River, 46; meeting the Shoshoni, 54–57; with the Salish Indians, 59; on Lolo Trail, 60; meeting the Nez Perce, 60–62; on the Clearwater River, 65–66; on the Columbia River, 66–67, 69–70; at Fort Clatsop, 73, 75, 78–80; return on the Columbia, 84, 86; with the Wallawalla Indians, 86–88;

revisiting the Nez Perce, 89–90, 92, 94; medical treatment of Pomp, 94; at Hungry Horse Creek, 95–96; recrossing Bitterroot Mountains, 96, 98; leader of southern exploration on return, 99, 113–117, 119; receives name from Cameahwait, 100; return to the Mandan villages, 121–122, 124; second meeting with the Sioux, 124–125; return to St. Louis, 126–127, 129; as Brigadier General and Superintendent of Indian Affairs, 130–133; marries Julia Hancock, 130; raises and educates Pomp, 130; on death of Sacajawea, 131; on death of Lewis, 133; forms St. Louis Missouri Fur Company, 133; as Governor of Missouri Territory, 133–134; appointed Superintendent of Indian Affairs by Madison, 134; marries Harriet Radford, 134; death of, 135

Clatsop Indians, 73

Clearwater River, 62, 65, 67, 92

Columbia River, 2, 4, 62, 66–69, 71, 73, 80, 85

Continental Divide, 33, 48

Cruzat, Pierre, 20, 30, 33–34, 68–69, 88, 110, 112

Cut Nose, Chief, 89–90, 96, 100

Discovery, 8, 26

Drewyer, George, 7, 27–28, 46, 49, 74, 94, 96, 100–101, 103–105, 121

England, 2

Experiment, 41

Field, Reuben, 43

Flathead Indians. See Salish Indians

Floyd, Sergeant Charles, 10, 94, 126

Floyd's River, 10

Fort Clatsop, 73–75, 80, 83

Fort Mandan, 17–18, 20–21, 26–27

Fort Osage, 131

Fort Union, 28

France, 2–3

Gallatin River, 44, 114

Gates of the Rocky Mountains, 43

Gibbon's Pass, 113

Gray, Captain Robert, 1–2, 4

Great Britain, 4

Great Falls of the Missouri, 34, 37, 41, 99–100

Grinder's Stand, 133

Grizzly bears, 28–30, 38, 101

Hancock, Julia, 130, 134

Howard, Benjamin, 133

Hungry Horse Creek, 95–96

Idaho, 4, 50

Janey. See Sacajawea

Jefferson Peace Medal, 7, 51, 56, 85, 100

Jefferson River, 44, 46, 99, 113

Jefferson, Thomas, 1–5, 8, 11, 20, 26

Jussome, Rene, 121–122, 124

Lemhi Pass, 48

Lewis, Meriwether: preparation for journey, 5–7; and Teton Sioux, 11, 13, 15; and Arikara Indians, 16; at Fort Mandan, 17–18, 21, 23; given nickname, 26; at Yellowstone River, 27–31; nearing Rocky Mountains, 31–32; at Marias River, 33; at Great Falls, 35, 37–38, 41; at Three Forks, 43–44, 46; on Jefferson River, 46; meeting the Shoshoni, 46–50, 53–55, 57; on Lolo Trail, 60; meeting the Nez

Perce, 60–62; on the Clearwater River, 65; on the Columbia River, 67, 69–70; at Fort Clatsop, 73, 75, 80; return on the Columbia River, 83–86; with the Wallawalla Indians, 86–88; revisiting the Nez Perce, 89–90, 92, 94; medical treatment of Pomp, 94; at Hungry Horse Creek, 95–96; recrossing the Bitterroot Mountains, 98; as leader of the northern exploration on return, 99–110, 112–113; encounter with Blackfoot Indians, 101, 103–106; wounded while hunting, 110, 112; return to Mandan villages, 121–122; return to St. Louis, 126–127, 129; as Governor of the Louisiana Territory, 129–132; death of, 133

Lisa, Manuel, 131, 133
Lolo Trail, 59–60
Long Knife, 26
Louisiana Purchase, 3
Louisiana Territory, 2–4, 127, 129, 131
Luttig, John, 131
Lydia, 80, 82
Madison, James, 133
Madison River, 44
Mandan Indians, 17, 24, 28, 116–117, 119, 121–122, 124–125
Marias River, 33, 99, 103, 109
McNeal, Private Hugh, 46, 79–80, 101
Minnetaree Indians, 24, 44, 49, 100, 114, 121, 125
Mississippi River, 1–2
Missouri Fur Company, 131
Missouri River, 1–2, 9, 27, 31–33, 41, 99, 106–107, 109, 114, 117, 124, 131–132

Missouri Territory, 133
Monroe, James, 134
Montana, 4
Muscleshell River, 23
Napoleon, 2–3
New Orleans, 2–3
Nez Perce Indians, 59–62, 86, 89–90, 92, 94–96, 104; as guides for Expedition, 62, 65–67, 69, 96, 98–100
North Dakota, 18
Old Toby, 57, 65
Omaha Indians, 11, 13
Ordway, Sergeant John, 114
Oregon, 4
Oregon Country, 3–4, 22, 55, 127
Osage River, 131
Osage tribe, 130, 132
Otter Woman, 20–21
Pacific Northwest, 4
Pacific Ocean, 2–3, 8, 69–70
Pawnee Indians, 11
Pomp, 21, 30, 34, 39, 92, 94, 113, 117, 119, 122, 124, 130
Pompey's Pillar, 117, 119
Portage: around Great Falls, 37–41; around Celilo Falls, 67
Potts, John, 43
Pryor, Sergeant Nathaniel, 116–117, 119
Pryor's River, 119
Puget Sound, 4
Radford, Mrs. Harriet Kennerly, 134
Rendezvous, 24
Revolutionary War, 2, 5
Rocky Mountains, 2–3, 21, 31, 33, 57, 59, 99, 104, 110, 115, 117
Russia, 4
Sacajawea: joins the Expedition, 20–22, 25–26; childhood in the Oregon Country, 22–25; meaning of name, 23; at Yellowstone River, 27; saves valuable papers, 30–31; at

141

Great Falls, 34–36, 39; at Three Forks, 44; at Beaverhead Rock, 46, on Jefferson River, 46; meeting the Shoshoni, 48–49, 53, 55–56; with Salish Indians, 59; on the Clearwater River, 66–67; on the Columbia River, 70; at Fort Clatsop, 73, 78; revisiting the Nez Perce, 92, 94; with southern explorers on return, 113–114; return to Mandan villages, 122; brings Pomp to St. Louis, 130; death of, 131

St. Louis, Missouri, 2, 6–8, 11, 18, 26, 33, 126–127, 129–130, 132

St. Louis Missouri Fur Company, 133

Salish Indians, 59

Scannon, 7, 32, 44, 83–84, 113, 119

Sheheke, Chief, 122, 124

Shields, Private John, 46, 48, 83

Short Narrows, 67

Shoshoni Indians, 20–24, 34, 43–44, 46–50, 53–57, 59, 65

Sioux Indians. See Teton Sioux Indians

Snake River, 62, 65, 67

Spain, 2, 4

Stray Away, 60

Tab-ba-bone, 47–48

Teton Sioux Indians, 11, 13–15, 122, 124–126, 130

Three Forks of the Missouri River, 44, 99

Tillamook Indians, 78

Twisted Hair, Chief, 61–62, 89–90

Two Forks of the Jefferson River, 113

Umatilla River, 66

Vancouver, George, 4

Vermillion, 49

Wallawalla Indians, 86–89

Walla Walla River, 86

Washington, 4

Washington, George, 5

White Bearskin Folded, 100

Wyoming, 4

Yakima Indians, 87

Yankee Triangle Trade, 4

Yellept, Chief, 86–87

Yellowstone River, 27, 99, 107, 109, 114, 116–117, 119

York, Ben, 7, 9, 16, 33, 40, 43, 129

Multiple copies of this book are available from:

The Caxton Printers
312 Main
Caldwell, Idaho 83605

Teachers

A FREE packet of teaching materials will be included with each order of 25 or more books.